Tropical Style

Tropical Style

Contemporary Dream Houses in Malaysia

by Gillian Beal
photography by Jacob Termansen
and Pia Marie Molbech

PERIPLUS

Published by Periplus Editions, with
editorial offices at 130 Joo Seng Road
#06-01, Singapore 368357

Copyright © 2003 Periplus Editions (HK) Ltd
Photos © 2003 Jacob Termansen

ISBN 0-7946-0021-2

Printed in Singapore

Distributors:
North America
Tuttle Publishing,
364 Innovation Drive,
North Clarendon,
VT 05759-9436, USA
Tel (802) 773 8930; fax (802) 773 6993
E-mail: info@tuttlepublishing.com

Asia Pacific
Berkeley Books Pte Ltd,
130 Joo Seng Road #06-01,
Singapore 368357
Tel (65) 6280 3320; fax (65) 6280 6290
E-mail: inquiries@periplus.com.sg

Japan and Korea
Tuttle Publishing,
Yaekari Building 3F, 5-4-12 Osaki,
Shinagawa-ku, Tokyo 141-0032, Japan
Tel (813) 5437 0171; fax (813) 5437 0755
E-mail: tuttle-sales@gol.com

contents

Malaysian dream houses

An advertisement by the Malaysian Tourist Promotion Board is playing on the television. While pictures of pristine beaches and traditional fishing villages on stilts skim by, the voice-over states, "I've found the best of Asia in Malaysia. Malaysia; truly Asia." Despite the cliché, this tag-line goes a long way towards illustrating how so many aspects of Malaysian life, including its architecture and interior design, draw on influences from around the entire Asian region, and indeed the world.

The quest for a national identity in architecture is a subject that has received much soul-searching. Malaysia is a modern nation with a diverse cultural heritage. Trying to define an identity in an environment where indigenous cultural forms vie with the forces of modernism and the latest international style trends, has been one of its main challenges. "What is Malaysian style?" is a question constantly being posed by architects and designers, new home owners, politicians, and the style gurus who define the modern culture.

In a multicultural, multiracial society such as Malaysia, the answer is, of course, that the style of the country is the sum of its many parts. It is an amalgam of centuries-old traditions and influences that have been assimilated throughout the country's long and varied history. "The interaction between foreign and indigenous ideas has provided the country with a rich architectural heritage, and the evolution of this has resulted in the development of an equally engaging contemporary architecture," notes Ken Yeang, one of Malaysia's most renowned architects, in his pioneering book *The Architecture of Malaysia* (1992).

Tropical Style is not an attempt at anything so daring—or controversial—as to define the style of an entire nation. It merely sets out to show how contemporary Malaysia is exploring its composite of multifarious traditions, and how architecture and interior design are contributing to the face it presents to the world in the 21st century.

Looking back, it is easy to review the making of a modern nation and list the various influences that have shaped the present. Malaysia is a country composed physically of two parts. The 11 states of Peninsular Malaysia, dangling like a pendant from Thailand in the north to the city-state of Singapore in the south, bisect the Indian Ocean and the South China Sea. The states of Sabah and Sarawak, located on the western flank of the great jungled island of Borneo, across the South China Sea, constitute what is commonly referred to as "East Malaysia". The numerous islands of the Indonesian Archipelago curve around the country.

It was Malaysia's location at the centre of the maritime trade routes between India, the Middle East and China—at the nexus of the monsoons—and the lure of its rainforest products that initially attracted traders and colonizers to its shores. In the early 16th century, the colonial powers arrived first in the form of the Portuguese, then the Dutch in the mid-17th century, and finally the British in the late 19th century. The latter dominated the country until independence in 1957. These colonizers, along with subsequent immigrant arrivals, have left an indelible mark on the demography, culture and architectural traditions of the country.

In terms of ethnicity, some 62 per cent of the country's 24 million people comprise ethnic Malays and other indigenous groups, such as the Iban in Sarawak, the Bajau in Sabah, and the Orang Asli in the Peninsula. A significant influx of Chinese and Indian settlers, brought in by the British to work the newly opened tin mines and rubber plantations in the late 19th and early 20th centuries, add to the country's racial diversity and to the variety, artistry and sophistication of its architectural heritage. The Chinese now make up around 30 per cent of the population and the Indians 8 per cent. Islam, the country's official religion, has contributed to the country's identity—and architectural mosaic—although other religions, ranging from Christianity to Buddhism, have played their role. These diverse cultural and social influences have come together in one giant melting pot within Malaysia, and many of the contemporary homes and hotels featured in this book look to these influences for inspiration.

The traditional Malay timber post-and-beam house is the foundation of the country's vernacular architecture. In his book *The Malay House* (1987), Lim Jee Yuan expounds its merits: "The traditional Malay house is one of the richest components of Malaysia's cultural heritage. Designed and built by ordinary villagers themselves, it manifests the creative and aesthetic skills of the Malays.... It created near-perfect solutions to the control of climate, multifunctional use of space, flexibility in design and a sophisticated prefabricated system which can extend the house with the growing needs of the family."

These houses, which are evident when driving throughout Malaysia's rural areas, are well suited to the tropical climate and the needs of their users. With the increasing urbanization of the country, however, they are faced with a serious threat to their survival. Fortunately, there are visionaries, such as landscape gardener Lim In Chong, who have determined to not only try and save them but adapt them to modern living. "The Malay building tradition is such an important and rich part of our cultural heritage, but sadly one that is fast disappearing," he says. As his house on page 50 shows, construction of a large timber house suited to the needs of a modern family is possible. Members of Malaysia's royal families, such as Tengku Ismail bin Tengku Su (page 60) and Tunku Vic (page 78), are also doing their bit to preserve the Malay vernacular house by reassembling, restoring and adding to original old houses. As Tunku Vic says, his house not only "highlights the achievements of Malay architecture" but also showcases "the creative and aesthetic skills of the Malays".

Malay timber houses are also the inspiration for two of the resorts featured in this book, the Aryani and Tanjong Jara, both in Terengganu. The Aryani has reassembled two 100-year-old traditional Malay buildings that were once part of the Terengganu royal palace complex in a bid to showcase the charm and simplicity of Malay vernacular architecture, while Tanjong Jara shows how its beauty can be incorporated into an international-standard hotel.

What has become more obvious in Malaysia is that an understanding of vernacular architecture is increasingly relevant to designing contemporary houses. As Frank Lloyd Wright has pointed out, "The true basis for the serious study of architecture lies with indigenous humble buildings everywhere. They are to architecture what folklore is to literature, or folksong to music.... Functions are truthfully conceived and rendered invariably with natural feeling. Results are often beautiful and always instructive."

The early foreign maritime traders who came to Malaysia's shores made no lasting impression on architectural styles, apart from introducing new types of buildings, such as forts and churches, the use of more permanent building materials, and rudimentary town planning. In the late 18th century, however, the advent of British rule led to the introduction of colonial architecture on a grand scale. Much of Kuala Lumpur's urban architectural heritage was built by the British colonial administration, and even after independence many expatriate architects continued to practise, and their influence is still felt. The four-storey walk-up apartment in Kenny Hills belonging to architects Frank Ling and Pilar Gonzalez-Herraiz, was designed by British architects BEP in the 1960s (page 218), while Richard Curtis has faithfully recreated the ambience of a black-and-white colonial bungalow from the same era within the Taman Duta district of Kuala Lumpur (page 150).

The immigrant Chinese and Indian communities enriched their new homeland with distinctive buildings, especially temples. The Chinese introduced sophisticated building technology, imported materials, and *feng shui* (geomancy) precepts. One of the most stunning examples of Chinese architecture in Malaysia can be found in the Cheong Fatt Tze Mansion in Penang (page 36). Painstakingly restored by architect Laurence Loh and his wife Lin Lee Loh-Lim, the project won a Unesco award for heritage restoration in 2000. Other properties featured show how Malaysian Chinese look to their roots for inspiration in the layout and design of their homes. Anthony Too, for example, has preserved his cultural identity within a 1952 two-storey Art Deco-style house in Kuala Lumpur's Golden Triangle by displaying his collection of Chinese porcelain, furniture and art. Indian influence can be felt in the Jayabalan home (page 176) which, despite being a modern tropical home, mimics the grand old houses of India with their colonnaded internal courtyards.

According to Gonzalez-Herraiz, the fact that Malaysia is on the whole very cosmopolitan, both politically and culturally, means that architects have to have an open mind when designing buildings. Indeed, no country can allow its architecture to stand still. As Malaysia became one of the region's economic success stories, its increasing affluence meant a new approach to architecture was required. As local architects took over from the expatriate firms from the 1960s onwards, the desire to establish a Malaysian cultural identity became more imperative. According to Lillian Tay, a partner with local firm Veritas Architects, who transformed a 1960s suburban house into an extraordinary home that is a study in space and light (page 106), architects have been struggling with the concept of expressing Malaysian style in their work for years now.

With economic success has come new wealth and the desire to build dream houses. According to Tay, adapting Balinese-style houses, where the owner can switch off from the stresses of everyday life, is a noticeable trend. She also says the work of Singapore-based Australian architect Kerry Hill is important within the Malaysian context. Kerry Hill is well known for his work at The Datai (page 120), which is a superlative example of building softly and sensitively within a rainforest site, but he has also completed several urban projects, such as the Ascott Building in Kuala Lumpur. Whether the desire to define a national style has been fulfilled is open to question

but what is clear is that there has been a move towards building residential properties and resort hotels that are suited to the extremes of the Malaysian tropical climate. The work of architects such as the Sri Lankan Geoffrey Bawa also had a major influence. As Ken Yeang explains, "For many of us ... Geoffrey will always have a special place in our hearts and in our minds. He is our first hero and guru." Bawa, a man who saw architecture as a means to give pleasure to all the senses and to create a unique sense of place, believed that "in a house in the tropics, an open-to-sky space must be the focus; permanently open, not peripheral or ancillary to the main activities".

The influence of Bawa and the Bali pavilion-style homes that offer open-to-the-elements climatic solutions to building design is very much in evidence throughout Malaysia generally, and within some of the larger homes in Kuala Lumpur in particular. For example, architect Kam Pak Cheong, when designing his house in the gated community of Sierramas (page 204), deliberately created a Balinese-influenced tropical resort home. "Whether we like it or not, we live in a tropical climate and we have to design our houses accordingly," he says. David Hashim, another leading architect, echoes this sentiment when he talks about his tropical home in Bangsar (page 136). "For me, a house is a place to relax, a place of escape. What we wanted to achieve with the design of our house is to create the feeling of being on holiday."

While acknowledging the debt of Bawa and Bali, Australian architect Gregory Dall of Kuala Lumpur-based firm Pentago, looks for a more timeless quality in his designs, employing a more classic architecture that he believes will not date. This is evident within his own home (page 196) and in the Jayabalan house (page 176) which his company designed in conjunction with the client. "Houses should be specially designed for living in the tropics," he says.

Others, such as landscape architect Ng Sek San, look towards the environment for inspiration. His futuristic weekend house (page 200), located an hour out of Kuala Lumpur, is essentially a steel and glass "glorified tent", a building that is informed by the landscape and treads lightly on the land. "We don't really have a Malaysian style at the moment," he says. "We are a unique melting pot with lots of influences." His mission in landscaping and building design, which he admits is not influenced by vernacular styles, is to throw out a lot of ideas in his work and to then test them. "If people like what we are doing in our work then they will copy it and that is how styles emerge." His philosophy of allowing nature to enter as well as to maximize air flow is echoed in the majority of places featured in this book.

Robert Powell, in his book *The Asian House* (1993) believes that often an identity crisis results in "regionalism" in architecture. "Regionalism is not simply the nostalgic privileging of the vernacular form but a synthesis of the vernacular with modernism. It is a way of thinking about architecture which is culturally regenerative—not a style, but a search for a cultural continuity in the aftermath of the colonial experience. It implies the embracing of modernism while simultaneously maintaining links with traditional forms and practices."

Wherever the argument ends, the houses and hotels featured in this book represent a celebration of Malaysia's extraordinary diversity and showcase a variety of approaches to the conundrum of creating a dwelling suited to a tropical climate characterized by intense sunshine and strong glare, high temperatures and humidity, and high rainfall and light winds. What they all have in common is a view that Malaysian style is not stuck in a cultural rut. It is constantly adapting, taking on influences and employing them in new ways.

Rather than Malaysians feeling that they lack an instantly recognizable architectural style, they should perhaps celebrate the uniqueness and richness of their manifold cultural influences. Variety is, after all, the spice of life. As Geoffrey Bawa has said, "I have a very strong conviction that it is impossible to explain architecture in words.... I have always enjoyed seeing buildings but seldom enjoyed reading explanations about them ... architecture cannot be totally explained but must be experienced."

Tropical Style is an attempt to provide the reader with the chance to experience some of Malaysia's dream homes and resorts, and by viewing the exceptional photographs gain an appreciation of the diversity of the country's tropical style.

tropical ethnic

Malaysia is a country rich in ethnic diversity, from the traditional tribal cultures of Sabah and Sarawak on Borneo to the many peoples who came to Peninsula Malaysia to trade, to settle or to colonize. Their legacy has created a cornucopia of design elements, be it the Malay timber house, the British colonial bungalow or the Chinese courtyard mansion. In this chapter, we showcase examples of these and highlight the ways in which ethnic elements are incorporated in contemporary Malaysian houses and interiors.

eclectic style

The house of Rolf Schnyder is a very atmospheric place that evolved over time and tells the story of his life in Asia over the past 40 years. Although Rolf moved to Kuala Lumpur in 1975 and started work on the house in the mid-1980s, it is filled with antiques, art and artefacts from his travels all over the region. The house, which is labyrinthine and constructed on many levels, was originally built for Rolf and his business partner, both bachelors. Rolf employed the services of architect Jimmy Lim, renowned for his timber houses, and the original structure comprised two wings with a central pool and living area. Later, when Rolf met his wife Chai, who is from Sarawak, he built another house of his own design for her on an adjacent piece of land, and connected the two places via a wooden bridge. When his partner retired, he bought out his share, and the house became a family home for the Schnyders and their three children.

For Rolf the most important element of the house is that the interior and the exterior are one. He wanted an open design, where water plays an integral part, and where the gardens are an extension of the living spaces. The supporting wood and concrete pillars have been placed within the central 2-metre (6.4-foot) deep swimming pool (right), while a sunken bar is level with the water's surface. The glass-encased wooden structure above the pool is the dining room, its sliding windows opening up to the night breezes. The pool not only connects the inside of the house to the outside but also helps to keep the house cool. A staircase leading up to the second house (left), decorated with old glazed European tiles from Melaka, is reminiscent of the stairs of traditional Melakan village houses.

Rolf, who has lived in Hong Kong, Thailand and Malaysia and has travelled extensively throughout the Asia Pacific region, has been an avid collector of antiques and artefacts for many years. He has an impressive collection of art, including works by two early expatriate artists in Bali—Theo Meier and Arie Smit. Rolf is fortunate enough to own a portrait of himself as a young man painted by Meier in 1962.

An attractive spiral wooden staircase with red accents within the dining room (opposite) leads to what Rolf calls the Eagle's Nest, which houses the guest rooms. From its balcony there are spectacular views of Kuala Lumpur and the landmark Petronas Twin Towers. The extensive use of wood is evident here, from the floorboards to the balustrades and a series of beams and joists. To one side is a wooden dining table surrounded by textured concrete pedestals on which are placed a variety of vases and other artefacts. The cushioned benches around the table allow for dining Asian style.

Indian patchwork cushions placed around a Khmer drum (above) form a casual sitting area within the main house. To one side is a 450-year-old carved wooden hardwood door from Bali. Behind some rattan-covered chairs from the Philippines (left) is a very rare tapered scripture cabinet from Thailand, carved and gilded with Buddhist motifs on red lacquer. On top of the cabinet sits an exquisite 170-year-old Buddha image. These represent just a fraction of Rolf's collection, testimony to his abiding love of the region he has chosen to make his home.

timeless elegance

The Aryani Resort, nestled on a 3.6-hectare (9-acre) site on the secluded coast of Merang in the state of Terengganu, is the brainchild of owner-architect Raja Datuk Bahrin, a member of the Terengganu royal family. A champion of Malay vernacular architecture, Raja Bahrin has constructed an intimate resort comprising 20 self-contained villas set in tranquil gardens. Although the resort's design inspiration comes from the sultan's palaces of old, the villas are contemporary in style and include all the facilities required of a modern-day traveller. There are two buildings, however, that hark back to another age. The Heritage Suite and the resort's spa are housed in two 100-year-old traditional Malay wooden buildings that were once part of the Terengganu royal palace complex. They have been lovingly preserved and possess an old-world charm that typifies the unhurried nature of this idyllic state on Malaysia's eastern shores.

The Heritage Suite (left)—which boasts stunning views across the South China Sea—comprises the main section, the *rumah ibu*, of a late 19th-century royal palace in Terengganu. Raised 3.6 metres (12 feet) off the ground as protection from floods, wild animals and enemy attack, with walls made of timber panels slotted into grooved frames, a steeply pitched roof covered in flat *Singhorra* clay tiles, and a broad covered veranda located at a lower level, it offers a glimpse into the climatic conditions and Malay feudal traditions which influenced its structure. A spacious day bed on the veranda provides a relaxing place to take in the view of the azure sea, while cocktails can be enjoyed on the lower deck while watching the sun set.

The resort's attractive swimming pool (right), surrounded by carefully manicured lawns and landscaped tropical gardens, features a simple *wakaf*, or pavillion, clad in weathered terracotta tiles. It is located between the resort's villas and the Heritage Suite, which is accessed through a gateway leading to a private garden.

The Heritage Suite comprises a master bedroom and a living room (left and above). The ornate woodcarvings above the windows and doors not only provide an attractive design element, but also permit a continuous flow of air so the interior remains surprisingly cool. Raja Bahrin had the luxury of having access to antique furniture from some of the old royal residences and he has used these attractive pieces throughout the suite. Simple woven rattan mats have been placed on the *chengal* wood floors, contributing to the simplicity and character of the accommodation. Yellow and green glass window panels create colourful reflections when the sun shines through them. Ceremonial umbrellas add a majestic touch, as do the cushions, covered in *songket*, the gold and silk woven fabric synonymous with royalty.

The master bedroom (above and right) is a study in the refined
elegance of a time long past. Full-length shuttered windows made of
solid timber panels open out to the private gardens, contributing to
the cross-flow of tropical breezes. The fine perforated carvings set in
the panelled walls and above the windows also allow air and light into
the room. Woven rattan mats soften the floor. The elaborate carvings
on the dressing table complement those on the walls. A dressing
gown and sarong, in a typical Malay batik design, provide splashes of
colour to the otherwise monochromatic room.

The simple white linen-covered bed is adorned with a piece of
songket, this time in yellow, the colour associated with Malay royalty.
Cream polka-dot mosquito nets, through which the tropical sunlight
is diffused, add to the highly romantic ambience. An unusual mirror
features an antique floral carving set within its centre. The rooms
deliberately feature sombre lighting to help recreate the essence of
a dwelling of the past which would have been lit by candles or oil
lamps. The Aryani Heritage Suite allows the visitor to experience a
wooden Malay residence completely attuned to the environment.

the blue mansion

The restoration of the dazzling cobalt blue Cheong Fatt Tze Mansion at 14 Leith Street, Penang, is a story of perseverance, preservation and passion. Laurence Loh, an award-winning architect, and his wife Lin Lee Loh-Lim, a heritage activist, spent 11 years lovingly recreating the former splendour of this mansion built in the 1880s by Cheong Fatt Tze, dubbed "China's last mandarin and first capitalist". Conforming to the layout of a model Chinese courtyard house, the mansion features an eclectic architecture that combines the myths and magic of the Chinese kingdom with the glory of the British Empire in the East. After acquiring the dilapidated mansion in 1990, the Lohs and a group of partners set about a US$2 million Grade One restoration, which resulted in the project winning a UNESCO Culture Heritage Conservation Award in 2000.

The two-storey mansion, surrounded by a 3-metre (10-foot) high wall, incorporates 38 rooms, 5 granite-paved courtyards, 7 staircases and 200 Gothic-style shuttered windows. Built on a symmetrical east–west axis, the building's design conforms to the principles of *feng shui*. The corridor-linked bedrooms (above) all look out on to the central inner courtyard (right) that also functions as an air-well. Two impressive wooden staircases either side lead to the upstairs rooms. The UNESCO award citation reads: "History was preserved by meticulously applying extensive research on the architecture, traditional artisan skills and materials to the restoration." The mansion stands apart for its fine decoration. Chinese craftsmen were employed to restore many of the design features, including the fine gilded carvings on capitals, doors and windows, and the colourful cut-and-paste porcelain shard work on the gabled walls, known as *chien nien* (left). Placed in juxtaposition, yet in harmony with the Chinese elements, are Scottish wrought-iron columns and railings, geometric floor tiles from Stoke-on-Trent, and English Art Nouveau stained-glass windows. All the furniture within the mansion is original—no reproductions were allowed—and is either on loan or has been donated by the antique collecting fraternity of Penang.

The Lohs' attention to detail in the restoration process is evident in their "restrained repair" of the elaborately carved and gilded timber screen that separates the main entrance hall from the central courtyard (left). A cautious and meticulous cleaning process was employed to gently remove more than a century of dirt and grease.

One of the outstanding features of the mansion is the decorative Victorian cast-iron work manufactured at the MacFarlanes foundry in Glasgow, Scotland. These fine, intricate pieces include the patterned balustrade surrounding the central courtyard (above and overleaf), topped by timber filigree carvings, and a spiral staircase (page 42).

富貴

Although Cheong Fatt Tze maintained several other homes in Indonesia, Singapore, Hong Kong and China, it is believed that The Blue Mansion was his favourite, which probably explains its extravagance. In completing the restoration of the striking porcelain cut-and-paste mosaics (top right)—whereby unglazed, coloured rice bowls are cut into shards with pliers and then pasted to form the elaborate patterns—the Lohs imported almost 10,000 bowls from Fujian province in China, and also brought in a number of master craftsmen. The indigo lime wash of the mansion's walls (left and below right), that gives it such a distinctive, intense colouring, is a replication of its original hue. This colour was widely used on buildings in Peninsular Malaysia in the 19th and early 20th centuries. In contrast, the four red columns on the first floor balcony at the front of the house denote the original owner's high rank.

The present owners of the Cheong Fatt Tze Mansion wanted it to become the living, breathing, people-filled building of Cheong Fatt Tze's time. They have therefore opened it up as an owner-hosted residential homestay with 16 themed bedrooms, all outfitted with period furnishings. Guided historical and architectural tours are conducted daily, while the ground floor halls and courtyard are used for special events. The mansion was also the site of the filming of *Indochine*, starring Catherine Deneuve. The film crew left behind three old rickshaws that now sit against a wall at the front, contributing to the grand journey into the past that the mansion evokes.

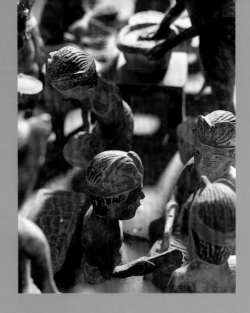

a collector's piece

More than 20 years ago, one of Malaysia's leading surgeons and his wife moved into what was once a simple developer's house in Petaling Jaya. Life has treated them well during this time, and rather than move to a larger property, they have decided to stay put. One of the reasons is that they feel they have been blessed with good *feng shui* in their home, the other being that they have moulded their house to fit their passion—collecting! Entire rooms within the house have been given over to thematic displays of Chinese and Asian artefacts and art. What was once a simple and ordinary house has been transformed through the addition of a veritable treasure trove of carved wooden doors and panels, Buddha images, ceramics and classical Chinese furniture. As their tastes and interests have evolved over the years, so too has the house.

The house is labyrinthine, with rooms hidden behind large wooden doorways. At the entrance is a broad, open terrace that looks on to the garden consisting of manicured lawns and a row of tall poplar trees planted over 20 years ago, each with a statue of Buddha underneath. The couple originally collected Chinese furniture and artefacts, which was "a matter of going back to their roots", they say. Later, they discovered the rich artistic and craft traditions of Indonesia, particularly Java, Timor and Bali. A more recent fascination has encompassed busts and statues of Buddha, and jade. They have also amassed a fine art collection, starting with traditional Chinese artists, then moving on to Southeast Asian artists. They particularly admire the work of Malaysian artist Cheng Fee Meng.

Separating the family dining room from the sitting room is an early 20th-century Straits Chinese screen from Melaka (left) depicting the four seasons. The end of an old wedding bed, ornately carved, decorates an open entranceway, fitting perfectly with the red tones of the room. An impressive 18th-century Shanxi elmwood door (right) from a nobleman's home leads through to the music room. Within the room is an old Shanghainese camphor bar that originally graced an old hotel. The painting on the far wall is by Malaysian artist Latiff Mohiddin, one of the country's top abstract artists of the 1950s.

The many Buddha images scattered throughout the house lend it an air of serenity. Although not practising Buddhists, the couple are deeply attracted to the image. On top of an old Chinese wooden stand sits an 18th-century Burmese Buddha in royal regalia (top). A tall statue of the Chinese goddess Kwang Yi, carved from a single piece of camphor wood, sits in front of a mirrored wall (above). Late 19th-century Chinese blackwood furniture, with mother-of-pearl inlay, makes up a formal arrangement in the sitting room (right).

The façades of four old Javanese wooden houses are strategically placed throughout. From the ample terrace at the front of the house (opposite), one set of beautifully carved doors leads through to the entrance hall. On the terrace coffee table is a large ironwood serving dish in the shape of a hornbill from Sarawak. In one corner of the banquet room (above), which can seat up to 30 people, sits a monolithic wooden statue of door guardians from Timor. Next to it is a 19th-century Chinese medicine chest of the type a physician would have used for house calls. On one wall is a series of door panels from Timor featuring kissing lizards (right). Wherever the eye falls, a carving, a statue, a piece of art provides a point of interest. The knowledgeable hosts are only too happy to tell the stories behind the many and varied pieces so artfully placed throughout their home.

a rural idyll

Lim In Chong is a man with a mission—to preserve the tradition of Malay wooden houses. These houses are a rich part of Malaysia's cultural heritage, but are fast disappearing. By building his house in Batu Pahat, a small town three hours' drive from Kuala Lumpur, Inch (as he is better known) wanted to showcase the beauty of traditional Malay wooden houses and, at the same time, demonstrate how they can be transformed into livable and comfortable homes. "I've liked wooden houses ever since I was a child, even though I grew up in a Chinese shophouse," he says. He is particularly fascinated with the variety of Malay vernacular house designs, which differ from state to state, and with the various species of timber used. The house which he and his family moved into two years ago represents something of an experiment for Inch. The heart of it consists of an original old house he found in Alor Gajah, near Melaka, at the entrance to which he has added new structures that recreate elements of traditional Malay house design.

The original house is a mixture of the Melakan and Negri Sembilan styles with a steep, curved roof, carved gable ends and a veranda enclosed by shuttered windows (left). When Inch found the house, it was falling apart. He dismantled it, carefully tagging, numbering, sketching and photographing the parts. "A lot of the timber was rotten," he says. He managed to save about a third of the original structure, including the walls of the veranda, some carved wooden panels, and the columns, in particular the most important one, the *tiang seri*. "The house was so far gone, I felt that I could experiment."

The reassembled and renovated house now serves as the entrance hall to the Lim residence, although in a traditional house this is where the men would sit. A ladder leading to the attic (right) is where young, unmarried women would sit and watch the men. The attractive carved wooden panels at one end are original, while the woven panels on the ceiling—more typically used for wall panelling—act as insulation and to cool the house. The floorboards are *cengal*, a local hardwood. The original house had very small windows, but these have been enlarged to open it up to the light.

Malay houses are typically small, although their basic design and construction methods allow extensions to be carried out whenever necessary. Inch has added extensive living and dining areas, a kitchen, bedrooms and guest rooms to the original structure, complete with traditional architectural details. Unusually for a Malay house, he has brought water into the house by creating a pond in the central area (above). The intimate dining area is open to the stunning gardens, allowing nature to enter. The beautiful timber used throughout is *seraya batu*, the same wood that was used in the original house.

The carved wooden doors that lead to the family quarters (left) are faithful reproductions of originals. Inch managed to find a 50-year-old Chinese man who, working with a young Malay assistant, had the necessary skills to complete these intricate carvings. The kitchen (right) is large, modern and bright with sheet metal used as covering for the walls. In Malay houses, the women's entrance is traditionally at the back, through the kitchen. Inch has retained this tradition by creating a patio and courtyard outside the kitchen that has become the informal entrance to the house and the one that the family uses.

In the interests of symmetry, Inch had a second house built parallel to the original old structure, and with the same dimensions, although it comprises two storeys in response to the level of the sloping site and to provide the space required for modern living. The internal areas were then created within the two structures.

There are four levels of privacy. The entrance hall is separated from the living and dining area by sliding doors, while carved half-doors (*pintu pagar*) act as a barrier to the more intimate areas of the house which include the family's private area and the four guest rooms downstairs in a separate wing. Each guest room has its own private terrace or garden (bottom right), in this case filled with an assortment of wild ginger plants.

Large wooden benches in the sitting area (above) overlook a garden designed to catch the eye with its flowering plants in predominantly pink and purple hues. Inch, a landscape gardener by profession, has also planted over 100 species of palms on the property, along with wild bananas and an array of heliconia. The house has been designed to maximize the free flow of air throughout with its tall roof, ample terraces (above left) and open spaces.

The house has been furnished with wooden furniture, an eclectic mix of pieces from the 1930s and 1940s interspersed with traditional Chinese blackwood furniture. The pool house next to the swimming pool features a column-free timber floor large enough for ballroom dancing, a passion Inch shares with his wife.

Sarawak style

Edric Ong, an architect by training, is a man who is passionate about the revival and promotion of the arts and crafts of the Malaysian state of Sarawak. His house in Kuching is testament to this passion, as it is adorned with Iban textiles, local ceramic jars and a plethora of ethnic woven rattan cushions and baskets. The house was originally built by Edric's father, Ong Kee Bian, in 1958, and was broadly based on the colonial civil service house plan for what were then known as Division One officers. Designed for tropical living, the two-storey property allows nature into the house at every turn. Sitting on a 1,000-square-metre (11,000-square-foot) site, the house is reminiscent of what Edric terms "ethno-colonial" style.

Edric describes the house as "cool, friendly, tropical and comfortable". He adds that the décor has developed over the years, and ethnic elements are mixed with some more traditional pieces that have been in the family for generations, including rosewood chairs and a sideboard. "I have very eclectic taste and so all the pieces are of different styles, but they seem to come together quite nicely," he says. Edric, who is a sixth-generation Malaysian Chinese, comfortably juxtaposes elements from his cultural heritage with the state of his birth. For example, his ceramics include huge Tang-period jars known as "dusun" and "dripping" jars that come from tribal longhouses. A large armchair on the terrace (left), formed from the root of an old tree, creates what Edric describes as a nesting place. The cushions and baskets are woven from rattan by Sarawak's nomadic Penan.

The inner living room (right) has bright cushions that cater to Edric's mother's preference. The carvings around the door jam are part of a collection of old Malay carvings from a bridal *panggah* or dais that date back 80 years. A collection of antique green-glazed ceramic jars are a focal point. Light filters into the living room, providing an atmospheric space in which to relax. One of the aspects of the house ideally suited to the tropics are the sliding windows. "I can open all my windows and bring nature into the room," says Edric.

Another sitting room (above) and the dining are (left) feature more local handwoven textiles and mats, as well as carvings and batik paintings. The guest room (not shown) has a modern touch but draws attention to exquisite silk Iban *pua kumbu* textiles that Edric commissions from Sarawak's weavers. He has not only brought this style into his home, but also into his work. His company, EO Design, produces eco-friendly products based on ethnic designs.

One of the most stunning features of the house is the extensive terrace (right) at the front which continues around one side. This is where Edric entertains friends and host parties. The floor is laid with ironwood planks, while the roof is made of lengths of *kaya seromah* wood, stripped of their bark, in imitation of the traditional construction of farmhouse roofs in Sarawak. Bamboo fish traps have been converted into light shades, while beaded baby carriers, tied to the backs of some of the chairs, add dashes of colour.

cultural perspectives

Although he grew up in the inner court of Dalam Kota, a collection of century-old houses within the palace grounds at Kuala Terengganu, it was not until he went to Japan as a 19 year old that Tengku Ismail bin Tengku Su's interest in the traditional Malay wooden houses of his birthplace was awakened. Impressed by the 300-year-old Ninjojo Palace in Kyoto that was originally built by Japan's first Shogun, Ieyasu Tokugawa, Tengku Ismail decided he would build his own wooden palace in Terengganu on Malaysia's east coast. He scoured the countryside for suitable buildings and brought together a collection of ten traditional timber houses. Eight were used to construct Pura Tanjung Sabtu, while two were dismantled to replace missing parts.

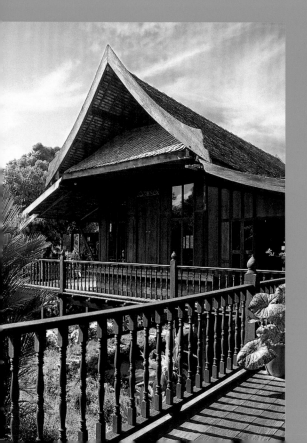

Between 1992 and 1996, Tengku Ismail moved the houses and re-assembled them on family land in a small village called Tanjung Sabtu at Nerus, 16 kilometres (10 miles) from Kuala Terengganu, the state capital. The 5.6 hectares (14 acres) of land form a peninsula jutting out into the Nerus River. The complex of eight separate houses, each between 100 and 160 years old, are connected by wooden walkways (left). A large house with 16 posts forms the main entrance hall and performance pavilion, while three houses are placed on the east and west wings of the central structure. Each house has the steep, tiered roof with curved gable ends typical of the region. There is balance and symmetry to the complex, which is open, maximizing its connection with the outside environment.

Tengku Ismail is a product of the historically close alliance between the Singapura-Johor and the Terengganu royal houses. The main sitting room (right) is filled with portraits of his royal relatives. Befitting his exalted heritage, his other great passion is for the gold and silk woven fabric called *songket*, which is valued for its artistry and detail, qualities that are reflected in the making of this house.

Tengku Ismail reassembled the houses using traditional construction methods in which *pasak* (wooden plugs) are used instead of nails. He was ably assisted by a team of local craftsmen led by Tok Ayah Teh Sar, a man in his eighties who possesses invaluable knowledge about the building of Malay timber houses. The entire complex rests on posts that place it 3 metres (10 feet) above the ground, aiding air circulation. Typical of Terengganu houses, the roofs are covered with terracotta tiles called *singhorra*, which are also found in Thailand and Cambodia, and are named after their place of origin, Songkhla, in southern Thailand. The wooden timber panels forming the walls are slotted into grooved frames, accentuating their rectangular pattern. The filagree-like panels above the windows and doors are finely carved using a piercing technique, to admit light and air.

The west wing of the house is devoted to Tengku Ismail's residence and includes his own private quarters, the main dining area (left), the sitting room and the kitchens. On the dining table, a piece of exquisite *songket* made by Tengku Ismail's own artisans is used as a table runner. The three houses on the east wing have been converted into guest rooms, available for rent. Here, visitors can enjoy a stay in a delightful residence that harks back to another era.

The interior design of the guest rooms is heavily Thai-influenced, which befits the area as Thai and Cambodian influences have shaped the culture of the east coast for centuries. Simple beds, either placed directly on the floor or raised on a platform (above), are covered in solid-coloured Thai fabrics. Colourful Thai cushions, gold temple umbrellas, Malay brassware and plain hanging glass lamps provide accents to the locally made furniture and wooden walls. The artistry of the woodcarvings is apparent as the light shines through them.

a house with a heritage

It is always sad when a house that has been part of a family for generations is put up for sale, but that is indeed the fate of the splendid Too family home in Kuala Lumpur. Built in 1952, this Art Deco-style two-storey house is located within the city's Golden Triangle business and commercial district, an area that is still graced with a number of grand old residences. The Too house, most recently occupied by architect Anthony Too, was built by his grandfather Too Choo Sun, owner of a printing business, Choosun Press. Too Choo Sun wanted to build a modern house for his family, and so called on the services of architect and engineer Y. T. Lee, who is probably most famous for the Chin Woo Stadium in Jalan Cangkat, completed in 1953, which is one of the finest examples of early modern architecture in the country.

Anthony Too was born in the house in 1957 and returned in 1985 to live there with his grandmother (who died in 1996) and an uncle, Tan Sri C. C. Too, a psychological warfare specialist. Anthony's grandparents had six children, none of whom lived in the house after they had left home as young adults. According to Anthony, the Chinese believe that a house only survives five generations, and "as we are getting to that point, the house has to be sold. It's sad. All my memories are from this house," he says. "My grandmother would have preferred not to sell it as she believed it should be kept in the family. But as there are now so many family members, the only practical thing to do is sell it."

The Too house, designed for tropical living, is set on a 0.2-hectare (0.5-acre) plot of land in which ancient flame trees and frangipani flourish. A large driveway leads to a commanding front porch. On the second storey is a spacious balcony, the setting for many family parties in the past. Little has changed in the Too house since it was built. It has retained all its original features, including the sea green glass windows, an impressive stair tower, and ochre terrazzo flooring, a characteristic of houses of that era. The Chinese blackwood furniture (left and right), collected by the family in the 1950s, has remained an integral part of the interior design.

In addition to being an architect, Anthony is passionate about Chinese culture. He is a keen collector of Sung Dynasty porcelain, Northern Song paintings and Ming-period furniture, in particular. Although much of his valuable collection is in safe storage, many fine pieces grace the house's living and dining rooms. Other artefacts from his family's past provide continuity. Above the small bar set in one corner (above), for example, is a letter to Anthony's grandmother from England's late Queen Mother congratulating her on her 96th birthday, while a portrait photograph of his maternal grandfather stares down from an oval frame (right) next to a hanging.

Anthony's respect for the past is evident in the interiors. The yellow colour of the walls gives the house an imperial feel, a colour Anthony says was his grandmother's choice. Previously the walls were white, which is not a good colour for the Chinese. Old Shanghainese crafts-men originally laid the ochre terrazzo floors and green skirting board, but sadly their skill has been all but lost in present-day Malaysia. According to Anthony, the rich colours create "a warm ambience, allowing you to sense the presence of the building". The 4-metre (14-foot) high ceilings not only aid the circulation of air in the heat of the day, but also contribute to the grandeur of the rooms.

a modern-day Malay palace

The Tanjong Jara Resort, located on the east coast of Peninsular Malaysia in the state of Terengganu, is imbued with the essence of its stunning locale. Opened in 1979, it was designed and built under the auspices of the Tourist Development Corporation of Malaysia with the aim of providing an example to local developers of how the beauty of Malay vernacular architecture can be incorporated into an international-standard hotel. The basic design motifs of the buildings replicate the grand *istana*, the elegantly crafted wooden palaces of Malay sultans of the past. The building won the coveted Aga Khan Award for architecture in 1983, when its designers were cited for their courage in seeking out and successfully adapting rapidly disappearing traditional architectural designs and crafts to meet the demands of a contemporary building.

The original consultant architects for the resort project, Wimberly, Whisenand, Allison, Tong & Goo from Hawai'i, undertook extensive research into the historical architecture of the area before designing the resort. They found that strong Thai and Cambodian influences in traditional east coast houses set them apart from those on the west coast. This is particularly true of the steep, tiered roof construction where the gable ends have carved edges and finials are set on roof ridges. These design elements have been successfully incorporated into the roofs of Tanjong Jara (above). When hotel group YTL took over the resort in 1995, a new swimming pool and restaurant were added and the public spaces extended.

Tanjong Jara is set on 17 hectares (42 acres) of extensive lawns dotted with coconut palms. It faces a beautiful stretch of deserted beach, with pristine golden sands. The resort's accommodation includes 10 single-storey individual cottages and 88 rooms divided among a series of two-storey buildings. Making use of native hardwoods, the buildings feature traditional carved elements created by local craftsmen, while their orientation ensures guests enjoy panoramic views of the South China Sea. The magnificent Anjung Suite (right) is set within a small lagoon on the edge of the beach, its carved balustrades reflected in the water as the morning sun rises.

The Malaysian climate and environment were also taken into consideration when the resort was designed. In the single-storey Anjung cottages, large windows open out on to the grounds, allowing guests to enjoy cooling sea breezes (above). Under the window is a comfortable day bed strewn with cushions covered in thick Indian cotton in earth tones. The colours harmonize with those of the terracotta pots in the public areas (right). The mixture of teak and *belian* used in the interiors adds to the rich, warm ambience.

island life

Pangkor Laut Resort is the sole occupant of a 120-hectare (300-acre) jungle-shrouded island situated 5 kilometres (3 miles) off the west coast of Peninsular Malaysia. The main attractions of this remote island hideaway, only a fraction of which has been developed, are the verdant 2 million-year-old unspoiled rainforest within which it lies and the stunning white sandy beaches which fringe its shores. Tan Sri Dato' Francis Yeoh Sock Ping, Group MD of the YTL Group, the resort's owners and developers, believes that "development can be in harmony with nature", a fact amply born out in the philosophy and thoughtful design of the resort. It imitates a traditional Malay village without sacrificing any of the luxuries that today's sophisticated travellers expect. The resort's accommodation, spread over two main areas—Royal Bay and Coral Bay—includes 21 sea villas and 22 spa villas set on stilts over the sea, 54 hill villas perched dramatically on the hillside amidst lush rainforest, 40 garden villas clustered around beautiful tropical gardens along the foothills, and 8 beach villas located within a few steps of a sandy white beach.

Bangkok-based architect Lek Bunnag and landscape architect Bensley Design Studios, who designed the resort in conjunction with YTL's in-house design team, were meticulous in preserving the island's natural habitat and jungle environment. The sea villas at Royal Bay (right) are especially attractive, mimicking the traditional fishing villages of Malaysia's coastal regions. Linked together by wooden walkways, they feature individual terraces (left) and bathrooms with windows on three sides that open up to refreshing sea breezes and views to Pangkor Island. Bamboo matting and plywood are used for the interior's ceilings, while shingles made from local *belian* wood make attractive roofing material. Muted colours and understated furnishings offset the richness of the timber interiors.

The spa village at quiet Coral Bay includes a collection of treatment pavilions, bath houses, gazebos and a lap pool in addition to the villas on stilts. Designed to soothe and refresh the senses, the various buildings face the sea, and are interspersed with open courtyards, lotus ponds, a herb garden and a reflexology path. The beach villas each include a private outdoor courtyard bath and shower.

At each end of the Royal Bay Sea Villas are the Purnama and Suria suites consisting of an entrance hall, separate bedroom (above) and sitting room (top right), with doors that open out to the sea. The ceilings and walls are lined with panels woven from bamboo strips reinforced with timber studs, similar to those used on the walls of the earliest Malay houses. The bed is covered in fine cream and white Indian cotton, with large "Dutch wife" bolster pillows. A day bed placed at the end of the main bed is covered with a bold ikat textile from Sarawak. A large vase filled with some of the exuberant foliage taken from the resort's gardens is reflected in the old-style swivel mirror. Wooden floorboards add to the beach hut feel. The simple décor of the sea villas adds to their relaxed, laid-back charm.

In the sitting room, a chaise longue made from water hyacinth stems woven over a wooden frame provides an ideal spot from which to take in the sea air while reading a good book. A welcoming sofa is made from the same materials, and both are covered with locally made batik fabric. A mat made of fine, split bamboo covers the floor.

The window behind the bed in the Purnama Suite (right) frames the wooden fretwork on the fascia boards, a feature prevalent throughout the resort's villas. Fretwork is also used as a decorative device on the walls of the bedrooms (left). Pangkor Laut Resort, with its offering of lush rainforest, idyllic beaches and an exotic mix of cultures, has prompted frequent guest Luciano Pavarotti to exclaim, "How beautiful God has made this paradise!"

living the Malay tradition

A still and quiet beauty pervades this traditional Malay wooden home built by Tunku Vic, a member of the Malaysian royal family. It is first and foremost a family home, but was none the less a real labour of love for the owner and his architect, Nik Ariff of local firm Gerakreka Architects, who spent eight years completing the project. "I wanted to build a nice family house, but at the same time wanted to highlight the achievements of Malay architecture," says Tunku Vic, "the creative and aesthetic skills of the Malays, and how Malay architecture suits the local climate and environment." Set in beautiful grounds, the property is made up of five separate houses joined together. The core is an old, reassembled Melaka courtyard house, around which have been built four other structures using parts of old houses from other states in Malaysia, supplemented by new parts based on old designs. The five separate houses are linked by walkways to create a peaceful home surrounded by jungle.

Among the key design features of the house are the carved wooden balustrades that surround some of the open decks (right), the perforated wooden panels above the windows and doors that create attractive shadows on the floors (left), the carved fascia boards fringing the roof eaves, and the decorative wooden gable ends. An ardent admirer and patron of traditional crafts, Tunku Vic has gone to great lengths to recreate original Malay designs that are in danger of being lost. For example, the fascia boards along the edges of the roof, which provide additional shade to the house, have been carved in a variety of traditional motifs, including the *kepala cicak*, or lizard's head (detail above). Moreover, the house has been constructed without nails, making use instead of the traditional system of joints and wooden wedges; in the past, this allowed houses to be easily taken apart and reassembled. "The traditional house builder seems inspired by the ordinary but with skill transforms it into art," he says.

For Tunku Vic, the main aim was to make the house liveable so that "you can hear your own thoughts rather than have the house dominate them". He strived to achieve the right balance, with "nothing shouting out". At the same time, he wanted comfort and a place that was "pleasing to the eye, the mind and the soul". The five houses form separate areas: a large, welcoming living room, a dining room, a master bedroom, the children's room and a guest suite. Each area is set slightly apart from the others, providing a sense of privacy.

According to Tungku Vic, the architect describes the house as a paradox. "It looks like the house of an extrovert, but really it is for an introvert as every room looks inwards. Essentially it is an expression of myself." Raised on posts, the house has wooden floorboards throughout which creak as you walk on them. The carvings on the panels and balustrades (left) not only provide decoration, but also allow natural ventilation and reduce glare, making the house remarkably cool in the tropical heat—a quiet, shaded haven.

Another notable feature of the house, used to great effect on the ceiling of the living room (left), are woven bamboo panels called *kelarai*. Although this is a rapidly dying craft, Tunku Vic managed to find an 80-year-old artisan who not only gave him a "bundle of traditional designs" but also managed to complete the beautiful panels on the ceiling of the master bedroom in the *raja beradu* (raja sleeping) design. The name of the design in the living room, which was woven by a younger craftsman, is *lampu empat pelitar,* or four lamps.

Penang's grand old dame

The grand, domed E&O Hotel at 10 Farquhar Street, Penang, ranks among the great historic hotels of the world. Originally opened in 1885 by the Sarkies Brothers—who also founded the Raffles Hotel in Singapore and The Strand in Rangoon—in its heyday, in the 1920s, it was the hub of social life in Penang. During those illustrious days, a parade of characters and celebrities passed through its doors, all keen to experience a lifestyle that epitomized the glory of the British Empire. Billed as "the premier hotel East of Suez" with "the longest sea front of any hotel in the world", it was a shining example of East-meets-West colonial architecture. When the hotel closed in 1996 for major renovation and restoration, local Penangites and fans of the E&O around the world waited with baited breath to see how the grand old dame would emerge.

The E&O's painstaking US$20 million restoration programme, which took five years, saw the grand hotel reappear in 2001, basking in the nostalgia of her elegant past. The elements of style and class remain, including the handsomely moulded arches and pillars, the domes and minarets that hark back to Islamic influences, the long seafront lawn, and the spacious domed lobby. The three-storey building, painted a gleaming white, has been positioned by the owners as an all-suite hotel "evoking an aura of place and time, maintaining strong historical links and traditions, yet coupled with the facilities of the present day". The feeling of going back in time is evident on arrival at the impressive courtyard entrance with its Victorian wrought-iron pillars and filigree work (right). A porter awaits at the revolving door dressed in a uniform complete with pith helmet, knee-high socks and gloves to usher guests into the spacious lobby and to an ambience that is reminiscent of the colonial days of Malaya.

The 280-metre (920-foot) seafront lawn and gardens that have so endeared the hotel to guests over the years have been maintained. Although the sea wall and embankment wall have been enlarged and heightened, huge waves still break over the walls during tropical storms, spraying guests. Within the gardens is an impressive swimming pool (left), enlarged during renovation, with its timeless palm-fringed sea views. Links with the past remain. A few old cannons, bought by the Sarkies from Penang's 19th-century Fort Cornwallis, point over the sea wall, while an ancient Java olive tree, planted before 1885, has been preserved. Even the linen and the crockery of the prewar E&O have been reproduced, such as the chartreuse-bordered cream tea set by Steelite of England (above).

The Sarkies brothers had a penchant for minarets, domes and cupolas, lofty airwells, columns, pillars and cornices that echoed traditional Armenian church architecture and harked back to their roots. This medley of neoclassical and Moorish influences is still very much in evidence throughout the hotel (left). The E&O was famous for its elegant steel dome—almost 16 metres (52 feet) in diameter above a tiled reception area of more than 186 square metres (2,000 square feet). Within its echoing confines, old Penangites would gather for afternoon tea in the hope of catching up on the latest gossip. Fully preserved, the echo beneath this signature cupola (above) is louder than ever, bouncing off the Carrara marble floors. Small openings within the cupola's surrounds allow natural light to filter into the lobby. The grand staircase has been recreated in all its glory, while the lobby's curved reception desk has been fashioned from Malaysian *nyatoh* and *merbau* timbers in the old style, complete with a wooden key box. Best of all, the original Otis cage lift, the first lift ever to be installed in Malaysia, is still in good working order.

The E&O's 101 suites offer either sea views across the strait to the mainland for those at the rear of the building or city views of historic Georgetown at the front. Some of the larger suites feature their own private garden terraces (above) complete with traveller's palms and spectacular vistas. The four Writer's Suites, named after famous E&O guests Noel Coward, Somerset Maugham, Rudyard Kipling and Herman Hesse, include a separate dining room and a lounge with a bar. The overall tone of the décor is eastern but with strong European accents provided by antique and reproduction furniture, including large wooden four-poster beds, Victorian-style wardrobes and dressing tables, and ornate writing desks. The sound of the whirling overhead ceiling fans when the terrace doors are open to the breezes makes it easy to imagine what it must have been like to stay in the hotel before the advent of air-conditioning. But the comforts that today's guests take for granted were not always provided. Many of the bedrooms of the old E&O had swinging half-doors (*pintu pagar*) that were installed to encourage the movement of air in the stifling tropical heat, but also resulted in compromised privacy. One English lady complained in 1924 of "sleeping very badly because … the man in the next room snored loudly all night".

The bathrooms of the E&O suites are both spacious and gracefully appointed (above). The chequered black-and-white marble floor tiles and scalloped-edge porcelain sinks with Beaumont brassware taps from Europe help to create an old-world charm. A wooden towel rack and a potted palm add to the colonial air. The fine linens are delicately embroidered with the E&O logo (right).

It is hoped that the newly refurbished E&O will engender the same loyalty and affection as it did in its previous life, perhaps recreating the sentiment expressed in a 1924 hotel booklet: "A short drive by rickshaw or motor car takes one to a hotel worthy of such a clime and of so much splendour of Nature. It is not, therefore, a matter for wonder that those who have once visited this famous Hotel, regard the E&O as a heaven to be sought again and again."

tropical fusion

One of the delights of houses in Malaysia is the sheer variety
in design and feeling one encounters both in the city and in
the countryside—a reflection of the nation's rich multi-cultural
roots. Be it a modern apartment with a veritable treasure
trove of Asian art and artefacts, a Balinese-influenced pavilion,
a hillside retreat reminiscent of British hill station cottages or
a luxury beachside villa, each home in this chapter represents a
smorgasbord of influences, styles and traditions. With Malaysia's
varied cultural styles, many elements from both East and West,
traditional and modern, can co-exist quite comfortably.

a many splendoured thing

Farah Khan, president of the Melium Group, Malaysia's most successful retail fashion group, was as strategic in her approach to choosing where to live in Kuala Lumpur as she is in making successful business decisions. Her 600-square-metre (6,500-square-foot) apartment is within the Kirana Kondominium at Jalan Pinang, an exclusive address in the heart of the city's commercial centre next to the landmark Petronas Twin Towers and Kuala Lumpur City Centre park. "As I once lived on the corner of 5th and 56th avenues in New York, I loved the idea of living within a huge park with gardens and water around," she says. She also enjoyed the fact that the apartment is "just minutes away from a six-star hotel, Malaysia's best shopping centre—the KLCC—a fabulous gym and world-class eateries." The Kirana's prestigious location is perfectly matched by its elegant design by internationally acclaimed Australian architect Kerry Hill.

Farah's latest venture is the retail outlet Aseana that produces and sells an eclectic mix of fashion, lifestyle and home wares sourced throughout the Asean region. It was a result of Farah's passion for collecting. "At some point I could not buy any more for myself. Now I put all the collections to good use at Aseana." Her spacious apartment is filled with antiques, paintings, carpets, textiles and furniture that she has gathered from all over the world. "I have been collecting all my life," she says, "at flea markets, auctions and country fairs."

In the hallway of the apartment (right), Farah's inimitable style is very much in evidence. Without employing the services of an interior designer, she has managed to create an informal and relaxed atmosphere for her collections. "With me it's a question of living among the things that I love," she says. On top of an old Chinese table is a cluster of Ban Chiang pots from Udon Thani province in Thailand that date back to 300 BC and were obtained at auction in Paris. To one side is an assortment of Javanese and Laotian drums. On the simple marble floor are a couple of small Tibetan carpets, while contemporary Southeast Asian paintings on the walls provide a colourful counterpoint to the earthen tones of the artefacts.

Farah's spacious living room (previous pages) features intimate arrangements of comfortable sofas for "interesting conversations". Bought in Europe, they have been covered in Cambodian, Thai and Laotian woven fabrics in warm colours—all within the earthy colour palette she favours. Large antique Turkish carpets cover the floor, their rich colours blending in perfectly with the rest of the room.

The impressive Chinese day bed in Farah's home office (left) made an appearance in the Hollywood movie *Anna and the King*. More Turkish carpets are complemented with throw pillows in shades of warm orange. In the dining room (above), a wall is filled with a series of Matisse lithographs, while contemporary dining chairs upholstered in deep red Thai silk surround a marble-top table from Indonesia.

According to Farah, she buys things that she is attracted to rather than thinking too much about how they will mesh with the other objects in her apartment. This goes a long way towards explaining her eclectic mix of furniture, fabrics and collectibles. But despite their different countries of origin, styles and ages, the individual pieces come together in a unified manner, with a sense of consistency and balance. At one end of her office (below), for example, a classic Chinese yolk-back armchair and a substantial Burmese teak cupboard are juxtaposed with a whimsical screen featuring signs of the zodiac. The textiles are also an unusual mix: an antique red Welsh blanket, a fine piece of Javanese fabric used as an antimacassar, and a richly woven throw from the Lebanon. A large armchair, made comfortable with plump cushions, provides an ideal place for reading. Picking up on the deep reds is a collection of Burmese lacquerware.

The large apartment, that boasts unrivalled views of the city skyline, has an interesting open layout. The breakfast area (right) receives bright morning sunshine, perfect for the start to the day. An attractive black-and-gold patterned screen from France breaks up the space. A collection of Sri Lankan betelnut boxes is laid out on an old Dutch colonial marble-top dining table. The cushions are covered in a bright Indian fabric. On top of a colourful, hand-painted Tibetan cupboard is an assortment of what Farah describes as collectibles, finding their rightful place within this highly individual home.

the far pavilions

Situated along a secluded bay on Pangkor Laut Island, off the west coast of Peninsular Malaysia, are the nine exclusive private residences that make up Marina Bay Estates. Together with Pangkor Laut Resort (see page 74–77), these are the only buildings on this pristine, forest-covered slice of paradise. The late Sultan Idris of Perak entrusted the island to its current owners, the YTL Group, in 1982, with the proviso that any development would be sensitive to the environment and leave as much as possible of the rainforest intact. The owners, along with architect Lek Bunnag and landscape architect Bill Bensley, took this to heart. Representing a loose interpretation of Malay architectural style, with the addition of other Southeast Asian influences, the residences recall the atmosphere of life as an estate manager of years gone by.

Sheltered within the rainforest and bordered by a private beach, each estate is a collection of individual buildings set within a landscaped garden. The five structures in these self-sufficient living compounds—which come complete with personal cooks and butlers—include living, dining, sitting, bathing and sleeping pavilions adapted from various Malay architectural styles. Each of the five main structures incorporates a different roof form. For example, the master bedroom of one of the estates (above) features an unusual octagonal wood-shingled roof, while the open sitting pavilion (right) is reminiscent of a Balinese open-sided pavilion. Here guests can appreciate the wild lushness of the forest setting while listening to the calls of the cicadas and the hornbills. It is testament to the landscapers and planners that these buildings have caused minimal disturbance to the natural forest; no trees over 15 centimetres (6 inches) in diameter were felled.

The private swimming pools (left) are the central focus of each estate. All are dramatically situated to take advantage of the best views, and all are different in shape and form. Wherever possible, the pools have been positioned level with the horizon. This, according to Lek Bunnag, is "the most powerful element of a beach resort".

The interiors by H. L. Lim & Associates, working with Jeffrey Wilkes and Richard Farnell, were designed, like the architecture, to reflect the lifestyles and resources of Malaysia and the region. Individual pieces pay homage to the country's diverse cultural heritage—such as the rattan wicker sofas and chairs reflecting the colonial tropical style—but have been given a strong contemporary edge. Fans suspended from high, wood-panelled ceilings in the pavilions are all that is required to provide a comfortable environment in the intense midday heat.

A natural palette of warm greys, wood and tan, ochre and gold defines the décor of the bedroom pavilions. Polished tropical hardwood floors add warmth to the muted tones. An oversized wooden platform bed (left) is the central focus of the room, its four posts drawing their design inspiration from a typical Malay house on stilts. The pillows and bedcover, made from raw Indian cotton in earth tones, include coconut shell buttons and seashells that continue the natural theme. The adjoining bathroom (above) bears the same natural tones offset by a brighter rug in a geometric design.

By limiting the colours of the décor, full rein is given to the brilliant hues of the landscape and the tropical garden. Although the different pavilions of each residence have varied roof forms, they are united through a shared use of materials, including local hardwoods, granite and sandstone, and Malay architectural details such as carved decorative screens and fascia boards fringing the shingle roof eaves. Many of the living and dining pavilions overlook the jade-coloured Strait of Melaka, while the secluded and private sleeping and bathing pavilions are wrapped in a mantle of jungle vegetation.

a study in space and light

In a quiet, unassuming suburb of Kuala Lumpur is the home of one of Malaysia's leading architects, Lillian Tay, a partner in the local firm Veritas Architects. It might seem slightly curious that a person who spends her time designing buildings for others should choose to develop an existing house rather than create a new dwelling in which she could give free rein to all her architectural inspirations and beliefs. Instead, Lillian has chosen to reveal her talents by transforming what was once a fairly ordinary suburban house, built in the 1960s, into an extraordinary home that is a study in space and light.

Lillian looked upon the work of modifying her house as something of a challenge. "The whole house was like an experiment for me, dictated by what it was like before, not by what I would do if I had a clean slate. In Malaysia, we have been ruthlessly destroying everything that is old in the belief that everything that is new is good. I wanted to see how—and if—I could work with the old." What she aspired to create was a feeling of openness reminiscent of an artist's studio. She has achieved this by removing floors and walls from the ground floor to create an enlarged living space (right) that now boasts 8.4 metre (28-foot) high ceilings.

It was also important for her not to overrenovate but to retain the essential qualities of the existing house. The tall windows that span both storeys have been preserved, giving the house an almost church-like atmosphere, as have the slatted windows typical of the period. But by replacing the original dark tinted windows with plain glass, she has allowed light to literally flood into the house. "Before I started modifying the house, it was very inward looking. So I opened it up by knocking out walls, expanding the size of the doorways and adding louvred timber doors—in other words, I opened up the space within the original envelope."

"I have never liked pompous houses," says Lillian. "I prefer something simple that allows you to enjoy the space, and with no unnecessary ornamentation." This is apparent in the décor of the house. Much of the furniture is of the colonial style of the 1950s. Lillian likes it for its sturdiness, although she says such pieces are getting more and more difficult to find. The dining table (left) has been stripped of its original formica top to reveal the stunning teak beneath. Morning light streams into the room, aided by the fact that Lillian has replaced some of the solid wooden wall panels with glass.

Lillian removed the original spiral staircase and replaced it with a simpler construction of cement and wood, complete with a modern metal and glass railing. The railing design is repeated around the boundaries of the second storey of the house (overleaf), creating a gallery-like feel. The high ceilings make the house perfect for a tropical climate as they act as a reservoir for hot air, reducing the need for air-conditioning. An unusual papier-mâché sculpture of a Malaysian dolphin, covered in colourful 1960s wallpaper, provides a conversation piece at one end of the living room.

A sitting area on the second floor (right) looks down over the living space below. Throughout the second storey, Lillian has added *berlau* flooring, a Malaysian hardwood that is as durable as teak but with a much quieter, more modern and subtle grain. In the master bedroom (above), Lillian has designed unusual wooden shutters. The curved slabs of wood, supported by metal poles, can be swivelled open to allow light and the breeze to enter, or closed flat to shade the room. Another feature of the Tay house is the modern art that adorns the walls, adding dashes of colour to the stark whiteness. Much of it is by young Malaysian artists whom Lillian is keen to support. Although these are among the modern touches Lillian has added to her home, she has no intention of making her house "too modern".

a riot of colour

The house of Bill Keith, one of Malaysia's leading fashion designers, in a quiet suburb of Kuala Lumpur, is a testament to his exuberant sense of colour and design. He has transformed this simple, two-storey house that was built 45 years ago into a warm and brilliantly hued home that positively vibrates with life. Bill is a man who does not believe that throwing money at interior design is necessary in order to get results, and his house is a shining example of what can be achieved on a limited budget but with unlimited imagination and flair. Using a palette of jewel-like colours, from sexy pink to lime green and gold, Bill's home is as individual as he is, and mirrors the originality of his stunning fashion creations.

The photographs on these pages capture a moment in the life of Bill Keith's interior décor. It is not something that is rigid and formal, but rather fluid and free. The man who only wears white says the house was once painted in the same shade, but the riot of colour we now see came about when he decorated to celebrate the Indian festival of lights, Deepavali. "Every couple of months I move things around. I love to change," he says. On the ground floor of the five-bedroom house is one large room that looks out on to the front garden through large glass sliding doors. Within the room there is a low dining table (left) and a comfortable sitting area.

At the entrance (right) is a console table that Bill designed and made himself. It has been created from three carved wooden panels from Sarawak. "I like to give my house that personal touch. I like being able to say 'I made this'." Above it sits an unusual wall hanging composed of a strip of tree bark from Sabah, the same material used in the traditional Sabahan bark cloth jacket and loincloth. The mottled effect on the wall was created by Bill employing the ragging method with a mixture yellow and gold paint.

The gilt mirror on the hot pink wall was picked up in Chiang Mai, in northern Thailand, while the lamp behind the simple sofa was found in Australia on an excursion to a flea market. "I travel a lot and always buy something, but whatever I buy I have to use. It must have a purpose," says Bill. Flowers are also very much an integral part of the interiors, particularly orchids, which Bill says he loves.

"I love to mix up the Chinese, Indian and Malay elements that are present in Malaysia," says Bill. "There's so much to show, so much to tell about these cultures." In the sitting area of the downstairs room, the Indian influence is very much in evidence. Purple voile curtains sway in the tropical breeze, while crinkled gold organza hangs from the window in the dining area. Many of the cushions are made of remnants from Bill's fashion collections. "I love bolsters and tassles," he says, "because they are so romantic."

Bill's artistic nature is evident in the way he sees his home as something akin to a canvas that he is continually adding to. The screen behind an oversized wing chair (right) is a case in point. Currently painted white with a gold tree motif, in previous incarnations it has been adorned with a sunset as well as a series of large banana leaves.

On the landing between the bedrooms (above and left)—each decorated in a different theme—are two slightly enigmatic portraits of Chinese women bought in a market in Shanghai for about US$20 a piece. On an old camphor wooden console, bought in Beijing, is a group of photographs of Bill and his family. The urn is an old pickling jar, used to make local delicacies like salted eggs, that Bill has painted.

The master bedroom (left) is as colourful as the rest of the house. The bedspread is a patchwork of Indian silk saris while the cushions are from Jaipur. The two lamps on either side of the bed, says Bill, are reminiscent of Kuala Lumpur's Petronas Twin Towers. Bill, who is a great admirer of birds, has hung a painting of a large Bornean hornbill behind his bed. The guest bedroom (below) has an Iban theme. The wall lamps are carved wooden baby carriers used by the indigenous people of Sarawak, while the "picture" over the bed is composed of a mounted collection of brass Iban earrings.

Although Bill has made his name as a fashion designer, his home is often used for photography shoots and has caught the eye of a number of people who have now called upon his unique and flamboyant style to transform their own homes and resorts.

high drama

Perched high above spectacular Datai Bay on the Malaysian island of Langkawi is the second home of Dr Peter Worm. A businessman and former racing car driver, who now raises sponsorship for the Lamborghini racing team, Peter is a man who lives on adrenaline. Upon returning to his native Germany after having lived and worked in Hong Kong for 15 years, Peter decided he wanted a place in Asia where he could unwind with his wife Manuela and baby son Nick. Villa Hutan Datai provided the answer. Designed by Kerry Hill Architects, the cliff-top home adjoins a series of similar villa properties that are available for rental or purchase, and are managed by the nearby Andaman Hotel. The Worm house is made up of six separate buildings providing 1,500 square metres (16,000 square feet) of living space on a 1-hectare (2.5-acre) steeply sloping plot that sits some 100 metres (330 feet) above a private beach.

Entry to the Worm property, set at the end of a private road, is through a pair of stone gateposts. Once inside the courtyard, the panoramic views across the rainforest tree tops to the turquoise waters of the Andaman Sea are breathtaking (left). The property's buildings consist of a living pavilion that seems to float above the land, a master bedroom overlooking the large swimming pool on one side (right) and, suspended some 48 metres (154 feet) above the jungle floor on the other side, a kitchen and dining room and three guest villas. Peter describes them as tree houses, but although wood is a predominant feature, he underplays their sophistication. They are built on posts to accommodate the steep drop of the site, which spans 50 metres (165 feet) from the villa's entrance to its lowest level. The buildings are linked by a series of walkways and paths, while an impressive wooden staircase—through which unfelled trees grow (above)—provides a focal point to the development.

Peter does not regard Villa Hutan Datai as a holiday house but more as a home. "I see it as a rainforest retreat," he says. The lifestyle in Langkawi is simple and laid back and, accordingly, these are qualities that the couple wanted reflected in their jungle home. One of the attractions of Langkawi is the rich and varied natural life of the area that includes 192 species of birds, 554 species of butterflies and 34 species of crabs, the perfect environment for Nick. "To bring up a kid here is fantastic—it's like living in a zoo," says Peter.

During his many years in Asia, Peter amassed a stunning collection of Chinese antiques and artefacts and these are displayed beautifully in the main living area of the home (above). The touch of Manuela, an interior designer, is felt in the quiet order of the room. The large sofas are covered in a fabric featuring Chinese calligraphy from a range produced by London-based company Andrew Martin Fabrics. The ornate, finely carved screen (left) that breaks up the room is over 600 years old and, according to Peter, came from the Forbidden City. On one side of it (above) hangs a 400-year-old Chinese opera costume in deep gold. "I decided to decorate our home in Chinese style," says Peter, "because of my love for Chinese culture and history, and all that is associated with the oldest civilisation in the world." The Forbidden City is a recurring theme in the room, with the story of the Last Emperor recounted in a series of paintings by Chinese artist Jiung Cuo Tang.

Outside the entrance to the living room, a pair of 18th-century elmwood Beijing official's hat style armchairs with cane seats (left) flanks a low cabinet-cum-bookshelf with brass handles. Large glass doors throughout can be opened to allow refreshing breezes from the sea to fill the room. The red *balau* floors have been inlaid with black marble slabs, creating an unusual contrast to the wood strips.

The Worms wanted to keep their island retreat simple and informal. The dining room (left), housed within a wooden pavilion, provides the prefect environment for relaxed dining. The room can be air-conditioned when the heat of the tropics gets too uncomfortable, but also allows for the doors on all sides to be opened to provide a more al fresco environment. An old square-drawer herbal medicine cabinet in the far corner is one of many Chinese items in the room, complementing artefacts from other parts of Asia.

In one corner of the living room is a fine collection of old stoneware jars from Sarawak, manufactured in China from the 10th century for trade with the island of Borneo. A chaise longue, covered in another Andrew Martin fabric, is an ideal place to lie, with the doors open, taking in the extraordinary sounds of the surrounding rainforest.

a touch of the Orient

Interior designer Jeffrey Wilkes and his partner Simon Gan are well known in Kuala Lumpur for their interiors shop, Ombak, in the Suria KLCC shopping complex, which sells exquisite home accessories and giftware crafted in many places around the Asia Pacific region. Their home is a reflection of the wonderful array of items that grace their shop. The house, which Jeffrey describes as "a box on legs", is unusual in that it is set on an extremely steep slope. The entrance at street level takes you into a living and dining area that has a balcony looking out over the gardens below. The drop is quite precipitous and the trees surrounding the property magnificent. "It is an oasis for us," says Jeffrey, "as we are surrounded by jungle, have very few neighbours, and feel isolated although we are only ten minutes from the city."

Jeffrey and Simon have been living in the 25-year-old house for the past six years. What attracted them in the first place were the trees, which give the sensation of living in the country. "It doesn't require a gardener. We just let the trees fill in the space." When they first moved into the house, they ripped out all the built-in furniture, straightened up some curved arches, and added slate floors. Then they set about filling the house with their collection of furniture, crafts and artefacts sourced from all over the world. "We buy things wherever we go. We are compulsive shoppers. We then put things we like together in the house. But the mood of the interiors goes in waves. It's always changing."

Sourcing items for the shop and for Jeffrey's interior design practice, the pair travel from Melaka to Sri Lanka, from Bali to India. The things they buy on their travels allow them to play with colours. In the dining room, for example, hanging over a teak dining table from Bali, is a pair of huge, circular, red lamps from Thailand. These were found years ago in a night market, and were made by blowing up large balloons and wrapping them with cotton. Matching their bright colour are the cushions on the oversized dining chairs, which are covered in hand-dyed, handwoven cotton fabric from Sri Lanka. Jeffrey likens their amazing colour tones to paintings.

When Jeffrey originally left Canada, he sold everything he owned apart from the things he could not replace, some of which have made their way into his current abode. A large leather sofa in the sitting room is from his country of origin. It looks completely at home next to leather armchairs from Shanghai and the other pieces from Asia. "I enjoy the variety of Asia," says Jeffrey, whose skill lies in mixing it all up into a style that can well be described as "Asian fusion".

On the far wall is a large, glass-fronted cupboard from Sri Lanka (above) that has been lovingly restored. It displays an eclectic mix of objects: Nepalese papier mâché containers bought in Delhi; an etching done by a friend; marble lions from Thailand; a framed piece of embroidery from Melaka; a Buddha image from SriLanka, and Jeffrey's aunt Betty's silver candlesticks.

The guest room and master bedroom (above) are on the floor below the living and dining area. Floor-to-ceiling windows look out to the forest garden, while timber floors create a warm ambience. The large variety of beautifully arranged decorative objects demonstrates what can be achieved with a designer's touch. A tribal Warli painting from Maharashtra, India, hangs over the bed, which is covered with a colourful patchwork bedspread, hand embroidered in Gujarat, a region famous for its textile work. The leather and wood armchairs are from Bali and the night tables from Melaka. The wool carpets were made in a factory in the Malaysian town of Ipoh.

From this second level, stairs lead down to an open area underneath the house where the supporting pillars are evident. It is an ideal space for large parties, as it is open to the tropical forest environment.

an individual style

When American businessman Dato' Kenneth Kolb and his English wife Sophie learned that this wooden house, built on two levels in the exclusive residential area of Country Heights on the outskirts of Kuala Lumpur, was for sale, they were immediately interested. They had admired it from afar, attracted to the fact that it took the traditional Malay house of the past as its design inspiration. They liked its individualism and its personality. After moving in, they spent three years fashioning the place to their own unique style. They stripped much of the local *cengal* hardwood used in the house's interior back to its natural state, added new wooden doors, built a swimming pool surrounded by lush landscaping, and constructed a large marble-clad dining room. The house is now a perfect reflection of their interests and individuality.

It was important for Kenneth and Sophie to have a house that was suited to the tropical environment of Malaysia. Having spent time on the island of Bali, they admired the way the outdoors becomes an integral part of the interiors of the houses there. "We like tropical architecture, and so opened up the house and incorporated design influences from Bali," they said. The swimming pool provides the focus of the spacious gardens, which the couple have landscaped with an array of palms and other tropical trees. "The plants cool the environment, and help create our Asian oasis." The pool is lined with black slate from India, while the two bronze temple dogs to one side are from Cambodia. A two-storey Malay-style pavilion, built from *cengal* and covered with an *atap* (thatch) roof made from split palm fronds, provides the perfect place to while away the days.

The spacious living room (right), lined with *cengal*, is a treasure trove of artefacts from the couple's extensive collection of Asian antiques. At one end hang hand-painted temple doors from Thailand. In keeping with the Asian theme, but providing a modern counter-point, is a portrait of Chairman Mao by American artist Andy Warhol (overleaf). The carpets on the wooden floors are Persian.

The couple's bedroom (above) is a calm and quiet retreat, a place where they can relax. A large four-poster bed made from coconut wood dominates the room. Above the bed is a calligraphic painting of *wah*, the Chinese character for patience. Doors lead to a spacious balcony that looks out over the gardens.

The attractive brass sink (left) in the bathroom is Kenneth's own design and is made from an old wok from Sarawak. Sophie, too, has stamped her personality on the house with one of the rooms turned into her boudoir (not shown). A romantic room, it is filled with beautiful fabrics, fine handmade Venetian lamps, and exotic Jim Thompson animal prints from Thailand.

A unique feature of the house is a secluded cellar area (left and below), a veritable secret hideaway. The entrance is revealed by sliding back a large gilt mirror hanging in the dining room. A glass wall in the couple's gymnasium looks out into the depths of the pool, providing an underwater view of the cool, blue water. A recessed room is decorated in grand Turkish style, with carpet-covered cushions, swinging hand-blown glass lamps and exotic fabric hangings and throws sourced from Istanbul's labyrinthine Grand Bazaar.

This is the place where Kenneth indulges his many passions. It is where he displays his fine collection of antique Khmer bronzes and stone carvings. He can be found here of an evening smoking a Cuban cigar taken from his humidor, drinking fine wines, sitting at the heavy wooden furniture that has come down to him through generations of the German side of his family.

reinterpreting Bali style

The house of David Hashim and his wife Asha is a reflection of their multicultural heritage. David's mother is American-Scandinavian, his father is Malay with Scottish-Chinese ancestry, while Asha is of Indian and Chinese parentage. With such diverse traditions to draw on, the Hashims did not feel tied to one particular style and their house is a veritable melting pot of influences, many of them Southeast Asian in origin. Their house in Bangsar, a busy suburb of Kuala Lumpur, started life as a 1960s bungalow. Rather than knock it down and build afresh, David decided to take on the challenge of transforming it into a place where he could escape after a stressful day at work. He set about adding to the original structure and developed a modern home that is reminiscent of the region's tropical resorts, some of which David has worked on in his role as founder and partner of Veritas Architects.

"For me a house is a place to relax, a place of escape," says David. "What we wanted to achieve with the design of our house was to create the feeling of being on holiday." The central living and dining room (left, right and overleaf) is the core of the original house. On to this core David has extended the house on both sides and at the front and back. As the house sits on an unusually large plot of land measuring 1,800 square metres (19,000 square feet), he was able to do this while still retaining an ample garden for his growing family. The house deals with the tropical condition within a framework of modernity. There are open areas that maximize cross-ventilation, covered terraces, wide overhangs, and a garden that is an integral part of the overall design. Befitting a tropical house, David has made extensive use of timber—the Malaysian hardwood *berlau* in the living room and Burmese teak for the floors. In order to give the house a tropical feel—which otherwise, he says, would have looked like a white box—he has added a wooden frame to the building's façade.

Every room in the house is carefully composed, testament to David's attention to detail. The Hashims are keen collectors and the pieces they have bought on their travels are grouped in a formal manner.

A collection of masks from all over the world looks down upon the living and dining area, which is separated by wood and glass partitions. Wood and glass doors lead out to a covered terrace where family members spend much of their leisure time.

An impressive staircase lined with terracotta and clay pots (right) provides the main transition into the house. Among the couple's collection of work by local artists is a painting of Asha dancing by well-known virtuoso of Indian classical dance, Ramli Ibrahim.

an island retreat

People build houses for many reasons. Rebecca and David Wilkinson built Tiger Rock on Pangkor Island, off Malaysia's west coast, to recapture the idyllic rural life they had experienced growing up in Kuala Lumpur in the 1950s and 1960s, and to share it with their three children. For them, childhood was all about running barefoot through the jungle, catching butterflies. David, a third-generation planter who had spent family holidays on Pangkor from the age of five, tracked down an old Malay man who had taught him to water ski many years previously, and asked him to find some land on which to build a family home. He found the steep plot on which Tiger Rock now sits. The Wilkinsons sold their house in Kuala Lumpur and moved to Pangkor to build what is essentially their dream home. "As we were building in Malaysia, we weren't interested in Thai or Bali style," says David. "Our influences were drawn from Malaysia itself—the bungalows of Port Dickson and Fraser's Hill and traditional Malay wooden houses.

The property consists of a pool house and swimming pool (left) on the lowest level, leading up to a spacious family home (right) and the Hill House for guests. Before deciding on the layout, David literally walked the land, getting a feel for its dimensions and topography. The 1.6-hectare (4-acre) site on which Tiger Rock is built has a steep gradient and is littered with large granite boulders. Rather than undertake any major earthworks, the Wilkinsons decided to build around what was already there.

The pool house (left) is reminiscent of the old-style plantation clubs of the couple's childhood. Indeed, the armchairs on the veranda were rescued from a club which was about to get rid of them. The bar was found in Melaka, while much of the furniture is simple and made out of plywood, but decorated with creative paint finishes and attractive stencilling by Rebecca. The two-tiered roof is made from zinc, covered with *atap* (thatch). The ceiling is lined with woven *bertam* palm used by the aboriginal Orang Asli of Perak. The pool looks out over a charming bamboo grove, which leads down to part of the forest reserve.

When it came to building the main house, the Wilkinson's were very clear about what they required. "We wanted a Malay-style house that was open to plenty of through drafts," said Rebecca. "Initially we thought the house could be built on one level, but when we cleared the vegetation we realized it had to be on three levels." The first level is the library (previous page), the second a combined living and dining room, kitchen (right) and bedrooms, while the top level is home to Rebecca's design studio. Building the house was no small undertaking. The couple had 2 tons of old teak floorboards and 1,000 tons of rock and sand brought in, along with an array of wooden window frames and doors collected from old houses and junkyards in Melaka. Their Malay builder, Pak Khalid, built the house by hand without the use of any major machinery. The overall effect is rustic and quirky, a house that possesses the unique and individual stamp of the owners.

One of the most unusual features of the house is the way the huge granite boulders form an integral part of the interiors. A large rock sits at the entrance to the dining area (above) while another has a bench built around it in a corner of the kitchen (overleaf).

Rebecca, who trained at Parson's in New York, has her own design company, Owen Rebecca Designs, which makes resort ware with designs based on the flora and fauna of Malaysia (above right). In Pangkor, she has the luxury of a spacious studio in which to work (right). The one-storey-building, overlooking a ravine, is surrounded by large boulders. The simple wooden doors were found in a junk shop. Rebecca simply cleaned them, and their original sky blue colour became the basis for the interiors of this inspiring space.

Rebecca's collection of old enamel tiffin carriers is displayed in the kitchen (above) and studio. The charming shell mobiles in the studio were made with her children. None of the windows in this rustic retreat contain glass. They are all designed to be thrown open to the stunning beauty of the natural environment, where the sound of the timid argus pheasant can be heard calling in the distance. Although the couple have undertaken some landscaping of the area, it is very informal, what Rebecca describes as "higgledy-piggledy".

For David, Tiger Rock is the realization of a dream. "I've always been interested in architecture. Having a go at it myself was always part of the dream, although to be honest I didn't realize how much work it would involve." Justifiably proud of the simplicity of Tiger Rock, he says, "I think it works quite well." Its naïve beauty, without formal architectural constraints, does indeed lend itself to a fantasy island home that sits at ease within the stunning jungle environment. Although the family lived at Tiger Rock for four years, they have since moved to Penang for work, and the delightful property is now available for rental as a laid-back holiday house where the jungle is central to the experience.

making the most of it

Australian interior designer David Winter of JWD Interior Design likens changing the décor of his house to changing his clothes. The interiors of his single-storey link house in Kuala Lumpur's fashionable Bangsar area, pictured in these photographs, capture a moment in time. Although the basics remain, the accessories constantly change. In his work as a designer of residential, hotel and resort interiors, David travels around the region—particularly to Sri Lanka, northern Thailand, Burma and India—collecting fabrics, furniture and individual pieces that he finds interesting. "I buy pieces that are well proportioned, well formed, and that I enjoy looking at. Although I can always use them on my projects, I usually buy them to keep, not to sell," he says. "I try to arrange a portion of my collection to suit the need at a particular point of time. In a period of a month, it will all change again."

The three-bedroom house in Bangsar is a small property that was originally built 27 years ago for Indian railway workers. It has a narrow 6.7-metre (22-foot) wide frontage and the entrance to the living room is straight off the driveway. The relatively small rooms could look cluttered with the addition of too many objects. David, however, has created a feeling of balance and harmony with a meticulous selection and placement of pieces within the limited space. Key to the success of the design is colour. "My colour palette has to blend from neutral to dominant," he says. "But most of the colours I use are earth colours, with brighter accents."

The living room (right) shows a small part of the extensive collection David has amassed in his 11 years in Asia. Standing in the corner are two tall satinwood columns that were rescued from an old Sri Lankan house. David also bought ceiling panels and a staircase from the same house, but these are currently in storage, waiting to play their part in one of his interiors. Sitting beneath an old teak coffee table from Burma is a Sri Lankan ebony stool. Two wooden decorative elements taken from the top of old temple columns sit on a table in the corner (detail above). On an old Burmese spindle (left), made into a table, sits a 16th-century Cambodian Buddha image resting atop a hand-painted wooden box from Sri Lanka.

David designs to suit his mood. In his bedroom (opposite), he has used strong red accents, ranging from rust and orange to a deep scarlet. The furniture is predominantly from Sri Lanka, and is made from dark, heavy ebony. The wardrobe is satinwood. The fabrics are from India and include a patchwork throw made from pieces of old quilts sewn together.

Within a small sitting area (above), a point of interest has been created with a blown-up photograph of a statue from the Arc de Triomphe in Paris. A satinwood and ebony dresser (left) is used as a bar. All the elements are brought together in a unified theme, providing a lesson on how to decorate small spaces.

reflections on the past

Most people when trying to recapture an era within a house have to resort to scouring antique shops and auctions to find what they need. Not so Richard Curtis. An avid collector with a family who has been in Asia for generations, he was able to draw upon his family's furniture and possessions of the past to faithfully recreate the ambience of a 1960s black-and-white colonial bungalow. When Richard decided to buy a house, he knew what he wanted. "I was looking for an old-fashioned house," he says. "I grew up in Kuala Lumpur, and when I was six we moved into a house in a new residential area. It had a feeling of fresh air, of openness, which was the tradition then." Although he was prepared to build his dream home, when he saw this old bungalow (which for many years had been used as a kindergarten) in the Taman Duta district of Kuala Lumpur, he knew he had found what he was looking for. "What I liked about the house was that it had an inherent charm and an integrity of design."

With the help of renowned Malaysian conservation architect Chen Voon Fee and his business partner Ruby Loo, Richard set about renovating and extending the house that had not been modernized since it was built in the 1960s. "The house had an existing personality, a soul that I was keen to preserve," he said. "Although it hadn't been abandoned, it had been neglected." Among the renovations, Richard put in new terrazzo flooring and a swimming pool (left), extended the terrace, built a new entrance, stripped the wooden floors, turned the garage into a library, and added black-and-white *chick* blinds. All the additions and restoration works were done in the style of the period.

An avid collector for the past 25 years, Richard has an impressive collection of 17th- and 18th-century lithographs of old maps that line the hallway leading to the bedrooms (right). The blank spaces on the walls indicate where he has loaned maps to museums and exhibitions around the world. A slightly more whimsical collection features antique birdseed holders (above).

Entering the Curtis house is like stepping back in time. In his bid to recreate the ambience of the 1960s, Richard has gone to great lengths, evident in the entrance (left). A granite rubble wall was added, as were typical terrazzo floors. The metal grills are copies of the original design and the furniture—which includes an old camphor chest and a planter's chair—is among that bought by his parents when they lived in Malaysia 40 years ago.

Different spaces within the house are used for different purposes at different times of the day. At midday, Richard sits out on the broad terrace, while in the heat of the afternoon he likes to retreat to the air-conditioned comfort of his library (below). The rattan armchairs are standard government servant issue typical of the era.

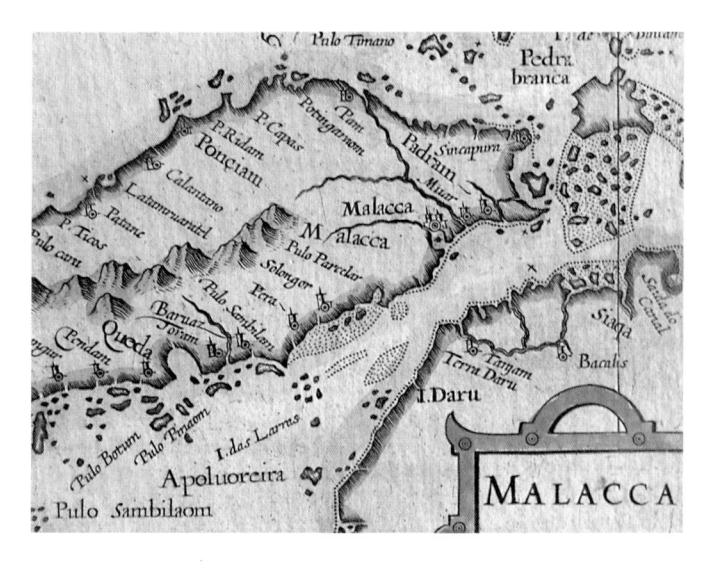

The furniture in the sitting room is arranged in a fairly formal style. Four Chinese horseshoe armchairs—bought by Richard's parents in Kuala Lumpur—are placed around a low coffee table. The collection of oriental carpets that are spread throughout the house belonged to either his parents or grandparents. Richard also owns collections of old silver, crystal and linens which come out when he is entertaining.

The house is airy and bright. "My intention was to live in the breeze, without air-conditioning," says Richard. His faithfulness to the period even extends to the plants. Around the pool area are heliconia, canna, frangipani and bananas—plants that were popular during the 1960s. At the front of the house, he planted grass. "When I come out of my house, I want to feel the grass beneath my feet," he says.

The guest bedroom (below)—which is fairly small, as was the norm in the past—is decorated in Oriental style. Above the simple bed, with its locally made rattan headboard, hang four carved wooden Chinese panels that belonged to Richard's mother. A collection of her antique embroidered samplers also grace the walls. Antique walking sticks lie across the candlewick bedspread, along with a pith helmet, a potent symbol of the colonial era. An old Malay silk shawl, laid across the foot of the bed, adds a touch of colour to the room.

Wherever you look in the Curtis house there is something to grab your attention. "A home has to be a home, and be comfortable," Richard says. "But people also need to be stimulated by what you have in the house, especially if you want them to come back again."

all in the family

Philip Yong has an historical and emotional attachment to the two-storey brick and timber house in which he lives in Kuching, Sarawak. His mother bought the land on which the house stands in the 1940s and asked Philip's father—the first qualified lawyer in Sarawak—to build her a house. They employed the services of an old Malay man named Abas, who acted as architect, carpenter and contractor in building what was then a two-storey wooden house typical of the colonial era. A few years later, Philip was born in the house. Over the next 30 years, the original structure went through many changes. Among others, a veranda was added and the ground floor bricked in. In 1973, Philip's mother bequeathed the house to him and moved into another house up the hill within the family compound. In the late 1980s, Philip undertook a major renovation of the property with his good friend, interior designer Rudolph Yap.

"Basically, we took the house back to what it was, how I remember it as a child," says Philip of the renovations. "We pulled down all the extensions, opened the courtyard which had been covered over, added new doors and windows in keeping with the period, and turned the car park back into a lawn." The house was completely opened up while retaining the shape of the original design. "We wanted to make it a comfortable, private home that suited Philip's lifestyle," says Rudolph. "I am a neat and tidy person. I like space and a well-ventilated house," says Philip. "Light is important to me. I hate dark, poky places."

An important feature of the house is Philip's impressive collection of Chinese pottery jars. Originally brought to the island of Borneo by traders from China, where they were exchanged for local goods, the jars have become cherished heirlooms in longhouses and homes. Historically, they are a sign of wealth for the tribal peoples of Sarawak and are still used for ritual purposes. In Philip's house, they are scattered throughout the rooms as well as on the spacious veranda (left). Complementing the robust pots is a collection of celadon pottery on a table in the dining room (right). A striking painting of a shell by a Norwegian artist, Ola Liland, a friend of Philip's, hangs above the table.

The spacious living room (left) demonstrates how the house has been opened up, creating light, airy spaces. "I love the house for its airiness and openness," says Philip. "It's not a place where you feel cooped up." To the left is the dining room, to the right the courtyard. No doors connect the three areas, thus allowing a free flow of air. The original ironwood staircase leading up to the master bedroom has been preserved. "Nearly everything in the house has either been made locally or sourced locally," said Philip. On the ample sofa is a handwoven *pua kumbu* "blanket", a highly prized Iban ritual textile, which has sentimental value for Philip as it was presented to him by the local tribespeople.

A 19th-century Chinese bench, purchased in Singapore, sits at the bottom of the staircase, beneath another Liland painting, this one of a coconut in the same complementary tones as the one in the dining room. This serendiptious harmonizing of colours happened despite the fact that the artist completed the paintings in Europe, unaware of the palette of the Yong house.

The master bedroom (left) is on the second storey of the house. It occupies a large space, as it originally comprised four rooms. The wooden floors, made of *selangan batu* hewn from nearby forests, are original. There are no air-conditioners in the room, but the many windows can be opened on a hot night to allow the tropical breezes in. Decorating the room are pieces that Philip has collected over the years, including more fine examples of his trade jar collection. Off the bedroom is a large veranda.

The open galley-style kitchen is perhaps the most modern room in the house and features imported tiles from Europe. The doors lead out to the lawns and there are partial views of the courtyard.

The courtyard, open to the sky, aids the cross-ventilation of the house. It has been laid with Chinese slate tiles imported from Singapore. It leads out to the large 1.6 hectare (4-acre) garden that surrounds the house, described by Philip as "a bit tropical in that it is rambling, and a bit Inigo Jones English". A restored antique wooden bench sits against the far wall of the dining room.

An ample terrace (below) wraps around the house, extending to the front entrance. Three Iban ironwood door stoppers in the form of pigs provide a whimsical touch.

tropical modern

Many of the architects working in Malaysia today are designing houses in what they call the "tropical modern" style. This means rejecting the air-conditioned, inward-looking dwellings of the 1960s and 1970s and embracing instead the earlier traditions of local vernacular and colonial architecture—but with a modern spin. These include blurring the distinction between the exterior and the interior to encourage open spaces, large louvred windows and sliding or folding doorways that provide more cross-ventilation, inside–outside gardens and pools, and a closer affinity with the natural environment.

space craft

Kamil Merican, a founding partner of award-winning Malaysian architectural firm Group Design Partnership (GDP), is a man who enjoys a challenge. When a plot of land in the residential gated community of Sierramas, just outside Kuala Lumpur, was considered too small to build on by the developers, he offered to buy it and they agreed. The fan-shaped site, measuring just 515 square metres (5,600 square feet), tested Kamil's architectural skills to the full, but his solution amply demonstrates that size does not always matter. Accustomed to living in apartments, Kamil designed the house to a simple plan: all the interior spaces flow into each other instead of being compartmentalized. He built the house to the land's boundary at the rear, despite its proximity to other houses, and placed the service areas there. The front faces a small, tree-lined avenue, and he took advantage of this by placing the living areas here.

The house is a modern home designed to suit the tropics. Large overhangs provide shade and protection from both intense sunshine and high rainfall, while a spacious veranda at the front (above) allows for outdoor entertaining. The façade (left) combines *berlau* timber panels and elegant steel columns. As the site lacked space for a coventional garden, Kamil created instead an impressive roof garden on the top storey, complete with palm trees, a vegetable patch and a water feature. It is protected by an iron railing that adds to the building's grace. One of the most defining features of the house is an internal light-well, a 1-metre (3-foot) wide slit running 10 metres (33 feet) from the roof to the ground floor. This floods the house with natural light. To ensure that this light filters down to the basement, which houses the laundry, a storage area, the children's playroom and the maid's quarters, a glass floor (right) has been laid within the light-well.

The first storey of the house, on a level with the road, comprises the living and dining areas, an open-plan kitchen and a guest room and bathroom. The master bedroom and the Merican's two daughters' bedrooms are located on the second storey, and are interconnected. All the rooms have sliding French louvred doors that can be closed for shade.

Kamil's wife Alia took charge of the interior design. Knowing that architects tend to favour clean, sleak interiors that can sometimes appear cold, she was determined to add warmth to the house. The mainly modern furniture has been softened with the addition of a few antique pieces. The colour palette is restrained, mostly pale sage green, pale gold and off-white. Light woods have been used through-out and include maple in the Italian kitchen and figured anegre veneer elsewhere, creating a more contemporary feel than the rich, dark hardwoods commonly used in the region. Kamil paid particular attention to lighting in the house, with the right mix of recessed, surface and spot lights to ensure the house was bursting with life. At one end of the house is a comfortable TV-watching area (right). Splashes of vibrant colour have been created with the addition of modern works by some of Malaysia's leading artists.

the art of city living

Landscape architect Peter Tan describes himself as the product of a Western education and Oriental sensibilities, a fact that is reflected in the décor of his home in Ampang, Kuala Lumpur. He bought the standard developer's house, built in the 1970s, a few years ago and has transformed it into a calm sanctuary. "I could see the potential in the fairly ordinary construction," says Peter, "in that there was a connection between the inside and outside." When renovating the house, Peter decided to let in as much light as possible. He installed glass blocks in the entrance, and then added sandstone slab floors throughout the first storey to unify the space. One of the main attractions of the house was that it had ample wall space for Peter's impressive collection of modern Asian art. His other passion is classic modern furniture, which, in his East-meets-West style, he juxtaposes with more traditional Asian elements, such as an array of Buddha images. "It's like going back to one's roots but living in the modern age."

Peter believes that the Malaysian art scene is a vibrant one that personifies the modern culture of the country. "Malaysian art is very exciting but artists here are highly undervalued," he says. The impressive, mainly abstract, canvasses displayed throughout the two-storey house provide much of its colour. "If you take away the art, the interiors are predominantly black and white," he says.

The house is built on two levels. The upstairs sitting room (right and overleaf) looks out on to a walled garden that is luxuriantly planted. The room has three areas: a formal sitting space (overleaf), a TV-watching area, and a relaxed corner "for chatting" that contains a black-and-white Le Corbusier-designed chaise longue. A strongly patterned carpet provides a dramatic contrast to the simple lines of the furniture. The large canvas, by Johor artist Ahmad Zaki, is a portrait from his "Man Smoking" series. According to Peter, it is an unfinished work, which makes it all the more interesting for him.

Peter has been collecting classic modern furniture for the past 25 years. In the sitting room (left), Mies van der Rohe's famous Barcelona chairs, stools and day bed are arranged around an Aileen Grey side table and one of her numbered edition rugs. Peter likes to layer things, to mix up the old and the new, and Western furniture with Asian artefacts. A 150-year-old *chofa*, or carving from the eaves of a Thai temple roof, provides a focal point to the main room. This piece is unusual in that it is covered in small mirrored tiles. As in the other rooms, the eye is immediately drawn to the art. On the left is a vibrant painting in oils by Arafi Ghani, while on the right is a black-and-white work by Nor Hanem entitled "Tropika". According to Peter, this artist is under appreciated in Malaysia and he has become one of his biggest supporters. Between the paintings is a tall beaded lamp by a French designer who lives and works in Vietnam. At night, the beads provide an unusual patterned shadow.

The two mounted figures (below) were bought in Chiang Mai, in northern Thailand. They are finials from a banister that are rotting away, providing an interesting sculptural effect.

Buddha heads and statues made from a variety of materials are a recurring theme in the décor. "They give positive energy," says Peter, "a serene and peaceful feeling when you enter the house." The large Buddha head placed in front of a vibrant yellow wall in the dining room (below) is an 18th-century piece from Burma made from papier-mâché. The contemporary dining chairs, designed by an Italian furniture maker living in the Philippines, are constructed from compressed and laminated bamboo. The rectangular lamp placed on top of an old Japanese *tensu* cupboard is available at Peter's Lotus Arté interiors shop at the Suria KLCC shopping complex.

The water garden (right) at the front of the house adjoins a large terrace used for entertaining. "The planting is very casual," says Peter, "using textures rather than colours, with bold, big-leafed plants providing a sense of drama." The pond is L-shaped and includes a water feature to produce the soothing sound of flowing water.

in the grand style

When Geeta Jayabalan and her husband commissioned local architectural firm Pentago to build them a house in Kuala Lumpur's Kenny Hills, they were clear about the brief. They primarily wanted a home that incorporated a separate area for entertaining and guest accommodation, an indoor–outdoor house where there was no boundary between the internal areas and the garden, and where water played an important role in the overall design. They worked closely with architect Gregory Dall and interior designer David Winter to develop their vision of a tropical home. In answering the clients' brief, and taking into account the steep, sloping site, Gregory decided to break the house up into three distinct areas: a lower ground area that contains the house entrance, guest suites, garage, wine cellar and audio-visual room; a spacious middle level that is used for formal entertaining, and a top floor exclusively for the family.

The Jayabalan home has a sense of grandeur, a sense of place. It is, above all, a well-ventilated tropical house with high ceilings, a stunning example of the indoor–outdoor concept of design. According to Gregory, the feeling he wanted to create was one of timelessness. Accordingly, the architecture is classic in style. Although the house does not scream Bali or India, the design influences of these two places are obvious. The 8-metre (26-foot) tall internal columns, for example, evoke the Jayabalan's ancestral past, mimicking the grand old houses of India, particularly in Tamil Nadu, with their colonnaded internal courtyards. The pillars add a human scale and break up the internal space, channelling people from the entrance to the inside.

The Jayabalans were keen to build a house that would showcase the Asian art and antiques they have collected over the years. As the house boasts 1,400 square metres (15,000 square feet) of floor space, both David and Gregory went on shopping trips with the couple to Thailand and India to buy additional pieces for their home. To one side of the ground floor sitting area (right), two impressive *chofa* carvings from the eaves of a Thai temple sit on either side of a 14th-century seated Buddha image. The house features many Buddha images, but they are not used merely for decoration, but are part and parcel of the family's spiritual life.

The internal architecture has been created using colours and forms that suit the Malaysian climate. The formal dining area (left) is predominantly white, with imposing windows that allow the tropical environment to enter into the grand, yet airy, space. A circular alabaster lamp, hand-carved in Spain, is suspended from the 9-metre (30-foot) high ceiling over the dining table. The table, which can seat 12, has a sandstone base and a glass top and was made in Malaysia. Much of the classic furniture was bought from galleries in Bangkok and Singapore, while the simple, elegant accents have been sourced from various places. To one side of the table is a *koi* pond that continues into the room from outside, adding to the cool ambience. The floors are laid with beige and white Italian travertine.

Through the tall windows, which are usually left open, guests can view the spectacular gardens. These are unusual in that they have been planted on a suspended concrete slab, essentially a false floor, to make them level with the entertainment area. A beautiful 28-year-old fig tree was brought on to the site by crane, while the balcony of the master bedroom looks out over a scented garden. A spacious outdoor pavilion adjoins the large swimming pool, and it is here that the Jayabalans invite their guests for informal drinks, and where they spend a lot of time as a family. Behind a row of pillars—of which there are 19 in the main house—is a pair of 19th-century red-and-black lacquered cabinets from Shanxi province, China (below).

The upstairs area, the family's private space, includes the master bedroom, three bedrooms for the Jayabalans' daughters, a meditation room, a television room and a large gallery that looks down over the centre of the house. To create a warm and intimate effect, the floors have been laid with fine Burmese teak. The Jayabalans' youngest daughter, Tasha, has a delightful bedroom (left) decorated in soft pink hues. The four-poster bed—like all beds in the house—has been placed according to *feng shui* principles.

The master bedroom (above) features wooden and glass doors that lead out to a terrace where two planter's chairs provide a relaxing place to enjoy the garden view. The 100-year-old, four-poster bed from Chiang Mai is covered in a silk bedspread from India. The carpet is one of many in a collection the couple have been amassing for the past 15 years. A Madurese day bed with interesting carved detailing (right) sits against one wall. The cushions are in Thai silk.

tropical minimalism

The owner of this family home in a quiet suburb of Kuala Lumpur commissioned Singapore-based Malaysian architect Chan Soo Khian of SDCA Architects to design and build a modern tropical home after admiring his work in an architectural publication. A Malaysian businessman, he had originally bought a colonial-style house perched on top of a steep incline, with a long driveway leading up to it. Rather than work with the original structure, he decided to demolish it and build anew. The result is an unmistakably modern home that is nevertheless rooted in the traditional dwellings of Southeast Asia, with its pitched roof, wide overhangs, courtyards, lush landscaping and the interaction between interior and exterior spaces. According to Soo Khian, the building of this type of house "presents an opportunity to explore ideas about preserving regional identity, reinventing structural solutions and refining architectural form."

"There are very few modern tropical homes in Asia, and I wanted to build one," says the owner. "I didn't want a house built in the stark minimalist style and equally I didn't want to build in the rustic tradition. So I specified our functional requirements and gave Soo Khian a free hand in the design with the understanding it would be a tropical house incorporating clean lines." The house has been developed to an open plan, creating a sensuous engagement with the elements. The steep site was modified and the house built on three levels. The entrance to the house is at road level and on this floor are the lower foyer leading to an outside courtyard (right), a wine cellar, office and study room. The living quarters and swimming pool are on the second level, while the bedrooms and private family rooms are on the third.

The entrance foyer contains contemporary furniture with curved lines. "We decided to bend things a little here," says the owner, "to make it a bit more feminine." The table by Finn Juhl and the Giorghetti chairs are placed on top of a woven mat. The tempered slatted glass screen creates an interesting prism effect when light filters through. "Balancing the sun and the other extremes of climate is an important consideration in a tropical house," says the owner.

SDCA's architectural designs strive "for tranquillity and calmness qualified by space, light and structural order", while capturing the spiritual essence of "place". In the sitting room (left), the extensive use of glass doors means that the landscaped exterior—also designed by SDCA—never seems too far away.

Throughout the house is SDCA custom-made furniture, such as the day bed and box lamp in the sitting room. Together with modern designer furniture sourced from Milan, the USA and China, it works well with the strict linearity of the house. In the entrance foyer (above), a series of works by Canadian artist Robert Berlin hang above a black lacquered Chinese console. Part of Berlin's "Asian series", they consist of photographs fused on to sheets of aluminium.

The sizeable swimming pool (right) is unusual in that it shares the same structural wall as the house since it had to be tucked on to a small piece of land. The master bedroom (left) is a quiet and peaceful retreat, with French doors leading out to a small terrace. The modern bed and side tables are by B&B Maxalto. A black hide carpet covers part of the timber flooring.

According to the owner, the house was built making extensive use of natural materials—wood, clay and stone—while concrete gels everything together. One of Soo Khian's signature design effects are the glass partitions placed between the top of the exterior walls and the roof (above). At night, when the lights are on, the roof appears to float. "This house will age well as it relates back to the environment," says the owner. "It's been designed to last."

a rainforest retreat

The Datai, on the northwestern tip of the pristine island of Langkawi, has set an unparalleled precedent in ecological resort development. Built on 750 hectares (1,850 acres) of untouched tropical rainforest and set above a secluded cove, the five-star hotel has its own white sand beach facing the peaceful Andaman Sea. Its 84 rooms are placed within four blocks arranged around a swimming pool that forms the heart of the hotel, and are linked by cool walkways, while its 40 villas are scattered among thick forest on the lower slopes of the site. Designed by Singapore-based Australian architect Kerry Hill, The Datai won an Aga Khan Architectural Award for its ecological approach: "The project attains a level of quality—both in terms of materials and experiences—rarely achieved in tourist developments. It is a successful combination of talent, stylistic refinement, attention to detail, the use of traditional forms and materials, and the rigour of modern architecture." The interior design, by Paris-based Didier Lefort and Luc Vaichere of Lefort-Vaichere Architects Associes, complements the sensitivity of the architecture.

When looking up from the beach, The Datai is almost invisible. A distinctive feature of the site is a ridge, set within the rainforest, that drops sharply down to the sea. Kerry Hill, committed to safeguarding the site's natural features, pulled the resort back on to the ridge to minimize the impact on the waterfront and to create spectacular views over the rainforest (left). The public areas—including the lobby, restaurants and a beach club—are housed in pavilions that draw their design inspiration from local vernacular styles. They also follow local traditions in that they are built either on posts or heavy stone bases with generous overhangs, design features necessary to accommodate the extremes of Malaysia's equatorial climate.

The resort's structure is integrated with its rainforest setting through the extensive use of local hardwoods. Wooden beams and railings are left unpainted and unpolished, allowing them to weather naturally, while columns of unplaned trees—felled on site—create spaces that seem like an extension of the forest (right). Maximization of breezes is achieved with spacious verandas that wrap around the buildings, and open pavilions and walkways. They also encourage an interaction with nature, blurring the distinction between inside and out.

Local woods are used extensively, picking up the textures of the hotel's buildings and the forest beyond. In the Dining Room, the resort's main restaurant, a wooden wall unit displays a collection of Asian basketware and pots. Within the voluminous lobby, supported by elegantly proportioned timber structures (right), two giant wooden horses on sandstone bases greet guests as they enter.

There are two swimming pools at The Datai, one at the beach club, the other just below the lobby in the centre of the resort (left). On a level with the rainforest canopy, this pool provides a peaceful oasis in which to soak up the sun or relax under generous white umbrellas. A Thai restaurant, The Pavilion, is a spectacular cantilevered building supported by tree trunks (below), its roof tiled with wooden shingles. The external walls of the main complex are clad in stone rubble (right), lending a monumental touch to the resort. The beach club is reached via a series of grand steps from the ridge to ground level and then along a meandering pathway through the forest. A series of rustic, thatch-roofed pavilions supported by timber columns surround the pool, home to the changing rooms and the informal restaurant.

There are 16 suites at The Datai, all located within the main building. Their interiors (left) feature warm red *balau* wood on the floors, around the doorways and in the panelling behind the bed, creating a rich and refined ambience. The lines of the furniture, which include a day bed for lounging and two comfortable armchairs, all covered in purple-hued fabric, are simple and classic. The pillows and bolster on the day bed are covered in finely plaited rattan, their two-toned geometric designs instantly recognizable as the work of the indigenous peoples of Sarawak. A handwoven ikat runner adds a dash of colour to the plain white linens on the spacious double bed. The unusual wall lights in the sitting room—created especially for the hotel—give the impression of fire torches. Scattered throughout The Datai's walkways and terraces are antiques, ceramics and artefacts from around the region that make interesting conversation pieces.

a house for the tropics

As an architect who has studied in great depth the vernacular traditions of the Southeast Asian region and who has designed tropical resorts and houses in Malaysia and beyond, Greg Dall had some definite ideas when it came to designing his own house in a peaceful suburb of Kuala Lumpur. Citing the influences of architects Geoffrey Bawa and Frank Lloyd Wright, he wanted a house suitable for living in the tropics that blurred the distinction between the indoors and outdoors, that made ample use of water, that was open and cool, and where the garden was interwoven with the building proper. His two-storey house fulfils all these requirements, but it is first and foremost a comfortable family home for Greg, his wife Kim and their two children.

When building the two-storey house, Greg wanted to make sure it was light and airy and had clean lines. "Tropical houses often use too much timber," he says. "When you live in them, they can be dark and heavy, and I think make you feel depressed." The ground floor of his house is spread over three levels: the entrance area, which has a guest room and a design studio for Greg; a dining area that looks out on to a reflecting pool and garden; and a family area (left) which consists of kitchen and living–dining areas and a staircase leading to the bedrooms upstairs. "It was quite a different matter designing this house compared to designing a client's house in that I know the end users very well. What we wanted to do here was to ensure that every space was liveable and workable."

A bright, airy feeling has been achieved with the use of high ceilings, an open-to-the-sky central area, white painted walls and neutral terrazzo floors. Wood has been introduced sparingly through the addition of old doors and columns from southern India. A large Gujarat door with clean, simple lines acts as a window from the family room out to the pool and gardens, while the columns, taken from an old Indian house, break up the large, open space of the dining room. "I like pieces that are different, that are works of art in their own right, but are also fairly neutral."

"The reflecting pool (right) is the heart, lungs and soul of the house," says Greg. "I find water, and the sound of water, very relaxing and therapeutic." This is where the garden is brought into the house, contributing to the cool and natural environment. The interiors of the house were designed by David Winter, who has used terracotta and warm green accents for contrast. "I like warm colours," says Greg. "They feel good." The house serves as a fine example of how modern design aesthetics can work within a tropical context for Greg to present to clients in his architectural practice, Pentago.

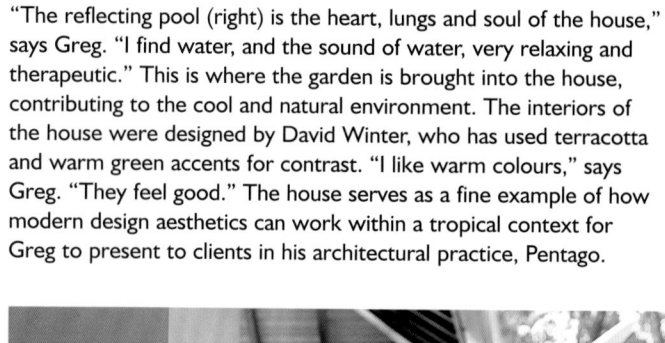

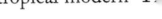

a simple forest dwelling

When Kuala Lumpur-based landscape architect Ng Sek San decided to build a weekend house in the country, he found a site on a steep slope in a forest, an hour away from the city centre, close to some Orang Asli (aboriginal) settlements. Rather than build a house that mimicked the traditional wooden dwellings of his neighbours, he opted for an ultramodern minimalistic house fashioned out of steel and glass that is exposed to the elements, and yet which incorporates the eco-friendly principles he absorbed when growing up in Australia and New Zealand. Sek San calls his house "a glorified tent" as it is transparent and open and treads lightly on the land. The house, which merges seamlessly and sensitively with the natural environment, is a study in simplicity and purity of design.

Sek San used the construction of his weekend retreat to test out ideas that he and his business partners had developed in the course of their work with Seksan Design. "The whole building is informed by the location," says Sek San. "We camped on site to get a feel for the land, to listen to what it was telling us, to understand the views, the sound of the nearby stream, and the way the breeze moves down the valley in the evening." No heavy machinery was used during construction and minimal use was made of concrete. Instead, Sek San and his colleagues resorted to using steel and glass, corrugated metal, and other mass-produced materials. "I believe that these materials are quite beautiful even though they are cheap," says Sek San.

The sail-like attachments to the house (left and right)—bought from a nautical supplier in Australia—not only provide shade and protection from the sun, but are also a metaphor for the house, "floating, sailing over the land". As the house is built into a steep slope, the entrance is through a sliding wooden hatch in the bottom of the house that brings you out on to the first storey—the living area. Encased in a dramatic glass shell, the boundaries between inside and out become blurred, the forest canopy greeting you at every turn. The floor of the spacious balcony (right) is made of industrial metal grating that would normally be used in factories. Its transparency allows you to look down on the lush vegetation and the stream below.

Furnishings are minimal in keeping with the clean lines and simplicity of this original retreat. The coffee table (above) is an old metal drain cover that Sek San recovered from a building site, placed on top of four railway sleepers. On the balcony, an old village wok serves as both fireplace and barbecue pit. A kitchen sink (left) is attached to the outside of the house, allowing the soothing sounds of the forest to mingle with the sounds of domestic chores.

An industrial metal staircase leads to the top floor, the sleeping quarters. A hammock and a simple mosquito net are all that are required in this camp-like dwelling that resonates with the owner's love of the outdoor life. The straight lines of the *damar* wooden floors find a reflection in the tree trunks that encircle the room. The house's simple bathroom reinforces the natural theme, with its compressed clay-brick walls and a floor strewn with river pebbles.

a tropical resort home

The design influences of some of the spectacular resorts that have been built in Thailand and Bali over the past 20 years or so have long been felt in Malaysia. The successful adaptation of vernacular styles in the creation of buildings eminently suited to life in the tropics is much admired, and in Kuala Lumpur there has been a trend in residential building to mimic these tropical resorts. One such house is the home of one of Malaysia's leading architects, Kam Pak Cheong, a director of BEP Akitek, who has been working in the field for the past 40 years. Pak Cheong has travelled extensively throughout the region and has been involved in the construction of a number of resort hotel developments. When he bought a plot of land in Sierramas, a gated residential community on Kuala Lumpur's city outskirts, he decided to bring these influences together to create a tropical resort home.

"Whether we like it or not, we live in a tropical climate and we have to design our houses accordingly," says Pak Cheong. In taking this belief as his starting point, he designed his family home with high ceilings and large windows that can open to the tropical breezes, maximizing cross-ventilation. He has also included terraces, open pavilions, verandas and water features throughout, while planting extensive gardens, thus merging the house with the surrounding natural environment and blurring the distinction between the interior and the exterior. "I wanted a house in which I could relax," says Pak Cheong, "a place where I could walk around in my shorts and feel completely at home." He has achieved this by building in a fairly minimalistic style, with restrained decorative finishing and the extensive use of wood.

The two-storey house is built practically to the boundaries of a 500-square-metre (5,500-square-foot) plot of land. The azure lap pool (right), built unusually on the second storey of the house, enhances the feeling of privacy. A Thai-influenced wooden pavilion with a terracotta-tiled roof is at one end of the pool, providing a comfortable place in which to sit and enjoy panoramic views of the surrounding jungle-covered hills. The ample use of plants in this open-to-the-sky area creates a welcome oasis of calm.

Water is a predominant feature of the house. A pond filled with *koi* surrounds the dining pavilion (left). When the doors are open, the space appears to float on the water, while the lush vegetation and water plants that surround it form an integral part of the room's ambience. Beyond the dining pavilion is a spacious terrace where the family spends much of its time. The interior décor is simple and relaxed. The walls of the sitting room (above) are painted a soft yellow. The modern furniture mimics the lines of 1950s pieces but in a pared-down form. There are no curtains as the plants provide adequate screening in front of the property's tall boundary wall.

Wood is one of the defining elements of the house, creating a rich, warm feeling. *Berlau*, a local hardwood, is used for the timbers and the roof of the pool pavilion, while the flooring in the master bedroom (right) is *merbau*. The master bedroom looks directly out on to the pool and pavilion. A simple day bed has been placed in front of the pavilion's louvred windows (above) which can be opened to the hillside view or provide shade during the heat of the day.

The furniture in the master bedroom is from Indonesia. A four-poster bed that traditionally would have been hung with netting to ward off mosquitoes has been left open. Pak Cheong says he likes the roughness of Indonesian furniture and its use of rustic timber. Balinese influence is apparent in the use of sandstone and carvings on the back walls of the pool, from which a waterfall flows. The glazed turquoise tiles that line the indoor–outdoor bathroom (left) are from Thailand and are the same tiles used within the azure pool. The grey sandstone that surrounds the bath is also from Bali.

a work of art

As one of Malaysia's leading artists, Dato' Ibrahim Hussein has received many awards and accolades from around the world. The son of a simple rice farmer from the Malaysian state of Kedah, Ib (as he is known to friends) has achieved much through an inspiring combination of persistence, courage and talent. Not content to live his life as a much-celebrated artist, Ib wanted to give something back. In 1991, he established the Ibrahim Hussein Museum and Cultural Foundation on Langkawi Island, a non-profit making, non-governmental organization dedicated to the promotion and advancement of art and culture. Housed within an impressive building designed by architect Lim Chong Keat, the foundation sits on a spectacular site within the Machinchang Forest Reserve, on land that was donated by the Kedah state government.

At one side of the foundation building, a long concrete path leads to a private residence built into the contours of the land, that boasts impressive views across the sea. According to Ib, the house went through an organic design and construction process. No machinery was used; everything was created by hand. The main living, dining and kitchen area (right and left) is essentially a simple glass-encased structure—a gallery-like space—with exposed wooden beams and a pebble floor. It is surrounded by a wooden deck overlooking large granite boulders on which the waves below crash. Much of the furniture and the unusual lighting (above) were designed by one of Ib's friends, Spaniard Ramon Castellanos, who is based in Cebu in the Philippines where local craftsmen make his designs. The room faces north, so the sun rises and sets across the vista. According to Ib, the colour changes throughout the day are mesmerising. "I am fascinated by the light," he says. "When there is a full moon, it is as if the whole island is lit up by a gigantic lamp."

On the far wall of the sitting room hangs one of Ib's paintings of his wife Sim and daughter Alia "whispering secrets". A coffee table has been created from a small wooden boat, with shell lights beneath a glass top. In the corner of the room is an ornately carved antique Chinese chair next to a whimsical statue of a donkey from Bali.

The gallery itself is set within 1,500 square metres (16,000 square feet) of space on two levels. It is an impressive structure that does justice to Ibrahim Hussein's extraordinary canvases. "To me painting is like praying," the artist says. "When I paint, I am dealing with my heart, my work, my God. There is deep joy and gratitude. Each piece frames a moment in my life." Gratitude is an integral part of the foundation as it represents Ib's "thank you to life". It is envisaged

as a living arts centre, one that will provide opportunities to struggling young artists while promoting the international arts scene in Malaysia. The gallery space, created by the architect as a structure possessing "clarity in form and space", is massive. The monolithic cantilevered staircase (left) is a feature straight out of the Bauhaus modernist movement. The high ceiling of the lower gallery (above) contains a large skylight that floods the space with natural light.

indoor—outdoor living

When interior designer Catherine Lai and her husband, advertising executive Tony Lee, bought a 1,400-square-metre (15,000-square-foot) plot of land in a residential area of Kuala Lumpur in the mid-1990s, they spent two years planning their ideal family home. Taking another two years to build, they created a modern tropical house that is intimate, yet is full of surprises. Having grown up in a country environment in Tapah, near the Cameron Highlands, Tony was keen to retain within their new city home the connection with the outside environment that is typical of village houses. The 372-square-metre (4,000-square-foot) concrete and timber house is U-shaped and built on three levels. Three sides of the house wrap around a central Balinese-style swimming pool surrounded by a large, informal courtyard with broad terraces and a pavilion.

The design of the house creates a smooth transition from the interior to the exterior. Large glass windows allow the abundant vegetation to literally invade the living spaces. Much of the house was laid out according to *feng shui* principles. A marble-clad water feature (right), for example, at the entrance is supposed to bring good fortune, while providing a cooling influence to the house. A large ceramic vase filled with a fine display of tuberoses adds an exuberant touch. Around the pool (left), carefully placed stone sculptures provide a Balinese touch to the landscaping.

Catherine designed all the interiors herself. She wanted the colours to relate to the hues of the tropical garden, and therefore chose a palette that is fairly neutral but with an emphasis on shades of green. Catherine often picks large palms and other plants from the garden, placing them within the house to bring the outside in. The interiors are contemporary in style, but include several antique pieces to add points of interest. "The interiors are not minimalistic," says Catherine. "A touch of romance is created by a few classic pieces of furniture. I didn't want the house to look too ostentatious. It's essentially a cosy home with accents of art."

Facing the entrance to the house is an impressive Burmese Buddha image set in front of a floor-to-ceiling panel covered in gold leaf with an antique finish. "This is our altar," says Catherine. "It blesses the house and there is nothing placed in front of it." The doors on either side lead to the dining room. Colourful accents in both the living room (below) and the dining room (right) are provided by works of art by local Malaysian artists. A large canvas by Fauzin, which represents his impression of looking down on the forest floor, hangs resplendent behind the spacious dining table, which is set for a formal dinner party with Daum crystal candle holders and fine glassware.

In the living room, a painting by Jai hangs over an antique Ming cabinet, traditionally used for storing food. On top of the cabinet is a parade of family photographs. The contemporary lines of the 80-year-old Chinese coffee table work well with the rest of the modern furniture and the foliage in the room.

a passion for design

Frank Ling from Sarawak and Pilar Gonzalez-Herraiz from Spain met when they were both studying at the Architectural Association in London. Deciding to collaborate both professionally and romantically, the two joined forces and established architectural firm Architron Design Consultants in Kuala Lumpur in 1994. They set up office in a four-storey walk-up apartment in Kenny Hills that was designed in the 1960s by British architects BEP. Later, when both their practice and their family expanded, they decided to take two apartments on the top floor of the building and combine them to create one large living space, while maintaining their office on the floor below. The design of the apartment is defined by two things: the fact that Frank and Pilar will have to return the apartment to its original state when they eventually move out, and their extensive collection of classic modern furniture and Malaysian art. As architects, Frank and Pilar believe that the design of a building should reflect the activities that take place there, while incorporating the spirit of the place. Their apartment is a fine example of these beliefs.

As they had a strict budget for the renovation, Frank and Pilar set up what they call "a simple logic of expediency". While knocking holes in the walls of the adjoining apartments to create a 230-square-metre (2,500-square-foot) space, they retained "memories" of the previous construction, such as a low dividing partition and the skirting board (right), which means you literally have to hop between the dining area and the living space. "We liked the idea that you can see the separation of space," said Frank.

The beauty of the apartment lies in the clean, utilitarian planning that was common to 1960s architectural design. Every room is bright, and with sliding windows leading out to a cantilevered balcony, the cross-ventilation is good. At every turn there is something to catch the eye. In addition to the furniture, the walls are covered with exceptional pieces of art, much of it by modern Malaysian artists such as Chong Siew Ying, Wong Perng Fei and Yilang. The furniture provides not only bursts of primary colour, but also reinforces the utilitarian theme. The colours of the Gerrit Rietveld red-and-blue lacquered wooden chair (above)—a piece designed in 1918—are answered in the Mondrian lacquered drinks cabinet (right).

Frank and Pilar have been collecting classic modern furniture since 1988 when they lived in London. Although some are pieces by the modernist designers who made their name during the early part of the 20th century, others are more recent. The colourful silk-screened satin glass lamp (left) was designed by Ferruccio Laviani in 1992 and can be bought from Italian lighting company Foscarni. The folding table by Giancarlo Piretti next to it is manufactured by Castelli. What all the pieces have in common is their renunciation of ornament and the use of geometric forms, qualities that add to their timelessness.

Frank and Pilar's pieces of furniture are not originals but are reproductions made by approved manufacturers according to the original, patented designs by such renowned designers as Eames, Mackintosh, Starck, Naguchi, Magistretti and Piretti. "Our furniture is like part of our family—we can't imagine life without it," said Pilar. In their work with Architron, Frank and Pilar hold a strong belief that "design is passion for, and a way of, everyday life". This passion for good design is evident in the everyday life of their apartment.

acknowledgements

The author, photographers and publisher would like to thank the following who opened their homes for photography: Richard Curtis; Gregory and Kim Dall; David and Asha Hashim; Dato' Ibrahim Hussein and Datin Sim; Lim In Chong; Geeta Lachmandas Jayabalan; Kamil and Alia Merican; Bill Keith; Farah Khan; Kam Pak Cheong; Dato' Kenneth Kolb and Datin Sophie; Khoo Salmah Nasution; Tony Lee and Catherine Lai; Frank Ling Lee Huat and Pilar Gonzales-Herraiz; Ng Sek San; Edric Ong Lian Bin; Rolf and Chai Schnyder; Shukri bin Shafie; Peter Tan; Lillian Tay; David Teh; YM Tengku Ismail bin Tengku Su; Anthony Too; YM Tunku Vic; Jeffrey Wilkes and Simon Gan; David and Rebecca Wilkinson; David Winter; Margaret Wong; Dr Peter and Mrs Manuela Worm; Philip Yong; as well as those home owners who wish to remain anonymous.

Our deepest thanks also go to the staff and owners of the hotels, resorts and restaurants featured in this book, in particular: Adrian Brown, E&O Hotel; Peter Bucher, Tanjong Jara Resort; Jamie Case, The Datai; Coliseum Café; Bill Dixon, The Andaman, Lawrence Loh and Lin Lee Loh-Lim, Cheong Fatt Tze Mansion; Old China Café; YM Raja Datuk Bahrin, Aryani Resort; Shook Restaurant; and Izan Yusuff, Group Director of Communications, YTL Hotels & Properties (Marina Bay Estates, Pangkor Laut Resort and Tanjong Jara Resort).

Special thanks also go to the following for their support during the preparation of this book: William Atyeo; Martin Axe; Soo K. Chan; Julian Davison; Guna and Malindra; Kim Inglis and Kevin McGrath; Leo Kuscher, Carcosa Seri Negara; Lim Teng Ngiom and Melisa Wong; Philip Marchione and Donna Wong; Frank Pinckers; Ian B. Semp; Donald Tan and Marina Foo; Uzma Nawawi; and Peter Wynne.